How to manage and teach

children with challenging behaviour

Veronica Birkett

Acknowledgements and dedication

I should like to thank the many teachers and teaching assistants who have attended my training sessions on behaviour management, from whom I have learned so much. My thanks also go to Peter Heath, headteacher at Blakenall Heath Junior School, Walsall, and all his staff for their valuable contribution to this book; to Debbie Pullinger for her wisdom and endless patience in editing this book; to Rebecca Barnes for her heart-warming illustrations; and to Cathy Griffin and all the lovely LDA staff for their friendliness, encouragement and trust in me as an author.

This book is dedicated to all teachers who have been irritated, worried, intimidated or even overwhelmed by the challenging behaviour of pupils, in the hope that the ideas offered here may increase their confidence and understanding of the issues involved. Teachers have my profound respect and admiration for the huge effort they often have to sustain in order to deal with increasingly high levels of challenging behaviour, while still managing to maintain high levels of success in academic achievement in school.

Every effort has been made to obtain permission for the inclusion in this book of quoted material. Apologies are offered to anyone whom it has not been possible to contact.

Permission to photocopy
This book contains resource sheets which may be reproduced by photocopier or other means for use by the purchaser. This permission is granted on the understanding that these copies will be used within the educational establishment of the purchaser. This book and all its contents remain copyright. Copies may be made without reference to the publisher or to the licensing scheme for the making of photocopies operated by the Publishers' Licensing Agency.

The right of Veronica Birkett to be identified as author of this work has been asserted by her in accordance with sections 77 and 78 of the Copyright, Designs and Patents Act 1988.

How to manage and teach children with challenging behaviour
MT10000
ISBN-13: 978 1 85503 400 6

Printed in the UK for LDA
Victoria Business Park, Pintail Close, Netherfield, Nottingham, NG4 2SG

Contents

Contents

Introduction   5

1 *Chapter 1*   7
       Challenging behaviour: the big picture

2 *Chapter 2*   17
       What is challenging behaviour?

3 *Chapter 3*   23
       Creating a positive learning environment

4 *Chapter 4*   33
       Managing behaviour with classroom strategies

5 *Chapter 5*   52
       Dealing with confrontation

Final thoughts   61

Resources   62

Introduction

Challenging behaviour means what it says: it is behaviour which challenges authority. It is 'throwing down the gauntlet'. In schools, the challenge will take the form of pupils breaking the school rules, or being disrespectful or abusive to those in authority or to their peer group. The vast majority of teachers and teaching assistants will, at times, encounter challenging behaviour which may interfere with their ability to carry out their very demanding roles. That may cause stress, anxiety or anger – or even become the reason why some choose to leave the job altogether. It is essential that all staff learn the skills to enable them to deal with challenging behaviour, and in addition that schools examine their current practice to establish that all possible action is being taken to prevent such behaviour occurring in the first place. If the school is inadvertently creating a situation that encourages or somehow colludes with dysfunctional behaviour, then teaching the staff behaviour management techniques will be largely unproductive. Every school has its own unique behavioural issues, and it is up to schools to identify just what these are and take appropriate steps.

Who will benefit from this book?

The aim of this book is to support both staff and schools in their endeavours to manage the challenge of disaffected behaviour. The book will be equally relevant to primary and secondary schools, and is written with the following groups of people in mind:

For senior management teams

- ◖ It defines their responsibility to provide a clear structure for the management of behaviour, in order to raise the confidence of the teaching staff and to support both staff and pupils.
- ◖ It emphasises the importance of establishing a positive ethos and learning environment.

For teachers

- ◖ It differentiates the 'troubled' and the 'troublesome'.
- ◖ It describes preventive measures for discouraging challenging behaviour.
- ◖ It enhances their knowledge of strategies and communication skills – the most significant factors in managing for good behaviour.
- ◖ It describes ways of avoiding confrontation and dealing with conflict.

For newly qualified teachers

- ◖ It provides ideas for a basic 'behaviour toolkit' with which to arm themselves in what may turn out to be their biggest challenge: the management of behaviour.

- It gives hope and reassurance that difficulties can be overcome and effective teaching can be learned: it is not simply a 'gift'.

For teaching assistants

- It will clarify their role in supporting teachers with general classroom management.
- It teaches strategies for use with individual pupils who present challenging behaviour.

For learning mentors

- It raises awareness of the issues which lead to challenging behaviour in order to create a greater understanding and empathy with pupils in their care.

For student teachers

- It will contribute to their success in the classroom by providing a greater understanding of the issues underlying dysfunctional behaviour.
- It will provide many strategies to enhance their efficiency and confidence when dealing with challenging pupils.
- It will offer examples of situations they may have to deal with in the future.

How to use this book

As the Ofsted report *Managing Challenging Behaviour* (2005) confirmed, there is little agreement about what exactly constitutes challenging behaviour. So we begin in Chapter 1 with an overview of how challenging behaviour has been perceived and what factors give rise to it. Then, in Chapter 2, we take a closer look at what we mean by the term, as well as establishing the difference between 'troubled' and 'troublesome' behaviour, and the implications of each.

Chapter 3 introduces a model for thinking about how to deal with challenging behaviour, and considers the steps schools must take in order to establish an environment that is conducive to learning and to limiting the incidence of challenging behaviour.

Chapter 4 deals with the practicalities of classroom management, offering strategies for creating a positive classroom environment and for developing healthy relationships with pupils.

Finally, Chapter 5 examines confrontational situations and suggests ways to avoid, defuse and deal effectively with them.

Chapter 1
Challenging behaviour: the big picture

"That's what I call a drastic measure"

Times they are a-changing?

Indeed they are. I have observed for myself, since the start of my own teaching career in the sixties, that challenging behaviour is now far more widespread in schools. It is also more challenging in its nature.

Discipline in the fifties and sixties

School life and the approach to managing behaviour was very different in the fifties and sixties. It was based on threat. My own personal experiences of school discipline at that time centred around the ruler, the cane and the strap. These objects appeared to be the mainstay of managing challenging behaviour. A 'beat it out of 'em' kind of approach, I suppose. How effective was this barbarity?

Food for thought

I only ever 'had' the ruler once as I was a well-behaved child, who always tried hard and was positively afraid of trouble. (Still am!) I can remember, even now, the horror of that early experience. I was 8 years old. First came the humiliation of being summoned to stand in front of the whole class, where 45 pairs of eyes were riveted to the scene. I had to hold each hand out in turn and two sharp blows were administered to each. It wasn't the physical pain that got to me, but the humiliation and embarrassment that I had been identified and found wanting; that I had upset the teacher and lost the respect of my friends. (I was a member of the 'good crowd'.) I can remember weeping, incurring further wrath from the teacher, who told me to 'get out' until the snivelling stopped. I think something may have died in me that day. At the same time was born some doubt about myself, or a belief that you couldn't trust other people – particularly teachers. An experience like that is bound to have a lasting impact and clearly it has. I can remember the scene as if it happened yesterday.

    I don't even remember what crime had elicited such a violent reaction. Had I dropped a pencil on the floor? Turned round in response to someone who had asked me a question? Smiled at the wrong time? Now, following my own many years of teaching, I suspect it may have been simply that this particular teacher had a row with his wife, arrived at school full of fury, and the first person to put a foot out of place became the recipient of the punishment he would have liked to have applied to his wife!

Being beaten with the cane was a big deal, and fortunately not an experience I ever underwent. The dispensing of this torture came under the authority of the headteacher. The expressions on the faces of the unfortunate pupils when they returned to class, their inability to write with bruised hands, or the obvious pain involved in sitting down served as ample warnings to the rest of us. I don't subscribe to the 'It never did me any harm!' point of view. I strongly suspect it did. Fear impacts on learning. The rigid boundaries established allowed no room for flexibility or individuality. Creativity was not encouraged. We fitted into a mould, and most of us accepted the situation without question.

When my own teaching career commenced in the sixties, corporal punishment was still up and running and, indeed, laws forbidding it did not come into force in schools until 1986. The use of the birch had already been banned in 1948, but it was not until 1998 that it was finally banned in the few remaining independent schools who had retained the practice. But back to the sixties: the instrument of torture employed at my school and in common use in the area (the Midlands) was known as the taws. This long, thick leather strap with a fringed end came into use on a fairly regular basis, often as a threat or warning.

Food for thought

My headteacher at the time would occasionally storm around the school, enter classrooms without warning and indiscriminately start beating the taws on the nearest desk. He would shout loudly that he 'would not endure such behaviour in his school'. We weren't always sure what behaviour he was referring to. I don't know who was more scared, my pupils or me. One thing was certain: there was no way any pupil of mine would be sent to the head to be at the receiving end of such fury. So straight away I had a problem – no support from senior management. Discipline was up to me, and for the next few years – with a minimum of 40 pupils in overcrowded classrooms, and few resources apart from textbooks, blackboard and chalks – there were inevitably going to be difficulties. And there were!

Hit the road, Jack, and don't you come back no more!

Life moved on, the head retired, a new head was appointed. I breathed a sigh of relief and hoped for better things. This head had an entirely different approach and didn't believe in corporal punishment. The taws was put in the bin, but his approach was an equally ineffectual one for me as a teacher.

Food for thought

A boy in my class at that time, whose name is etched in my memory for ever because of his frequent off-the-wall behaviour, one day went too far. I decided to send him to the head, safe in the knowledge that he wouldn't receive a beating, as in the old days. He was away for some time, and I imagined him being lectured sternly, then returning a reformed character. He returned – with a nice red school pencil. It was a bribe from the head, who had told him that if he behaved for me he could have this pencil. The effect on the rest of the class was immediate. The 'hard core' kicked off, also hoping for the visit and the red pencil. Red pencils were a big deal in those days. Money was short and red pencils were a treat, especially as they had the school name engraved on them. So now we had discipline supported by bribes. Offenders loved these visits, which were of course a treat, not a sanction, so I soon stopped sending them. On my own again.

Neither corporal punishment nor Mr Nice Guy worked for me. So what happened next?

You got to accentuate the positive, eliminate the negative

In 1989, Lord Elton chaired the Committee of Enquiry into Discipline in schools, and the ensuing report indicated that schools which were preoccupied with bad behaviour were far less successful than schools that adopted an orderly and positive approach. This was to be established by:

- providing positive role models in teachers;
- promoting high expectations of all pupils;
- ensuring the staff worked together consistently for the benefit of pupils;
- establishing an effective behaviour policy to be followed by all;
- employing a key teacher who understood the nature of behavioural and emotional difficulties;

○ working with a suitably challenging curriculum;

○ providing opportunities for pupils to learn from their own actions.

The Elton Committee certainly supported the banning of corporal punishment, and saw its use as encouraging a negative, reactive approach, rather than the positive, proactive one they recommended as a result of their research.

The report must have had a powerful effect because the 1990s saw a rapid growth in schools choosing to make use of 'assertive discipline'. The original concept came from Lee Canter, an American whose books and training programmes became very popular at that time. The basic idea was that schools should focus on reward rather than punishment. This positive approach, in line with the Elton recommendations, was achieved by training teachers to take an assertive stance, which involved establishing a few classroom rules with firm, clear directions for pupils about what was expected and what the consequences would be if rules were not followed. Many schools found this approach had a significant general impact, but it was obviously not a complete solution; the numbers of pupils permanently excluded from schools rose dramatically from 2,910 in 1990/1 to 12,700 in 1997/8. As a result, Pupil Referral Units (PRUs) were established in 1997 for 'at risk' pupils. It was hoped the pupils attending them would learn ways of coping and soon return to mainstream education.

One of the reasons for this growth in exclusion has been the government policy to promote, whenever possible, the inclusion of pupils who have special educational needs (SEN) in mainstream schools. This includes those with emotional, behavioural and social difficulties (EBSD), and means that teachers were given the responsibility of managing some very disruptive pupils. There are consequences. The Ofsted report *Managing Challenging Behaviour* (2005) stated that there was a 25 per cent increase between 2001 and 2003 in pupils placed in PRUs. In addition, there was a 14 per cent increase in the numbers of pupils with EBSD placed in independent special schools. The report confirms the commonly held view that it is this particular group of pupils that teachers find the most challenging. Taking a 'positive approach' is not necessarily a cure-all.

The management of disruptive behaviour has now become a significant problem, with the Department for Education and Skills (DfES) providing substantial funding to schools with a high proportion of pupils presenting, or likely to develop, disruptive behaviour, in an attempt to support such schools and alleviate the issue. Behaviour in secondary schools is a particular concern. In 1996/7, overall behaviour in schools was judged good or better by Ofsted in three quarters of schools, but in 2003/4 the proportion had increased to almost two thirds.

Survival of the fittest – and the not so fit

Workload and poor pupil behaviour have been identified as the key reasons why many teachers leave the profession. However, some teachers who find the management of behaviour difficult simply stay put because they feel it is too late to change careers or because they see no other option available. So, what happens in situations where schools have failed to establish an effective support system, or where teachers' skills fail to meet the challenge of dealing with difficult behaviour?

Schools will:

- experience falling rolls;
- attract pupils who have been excluded from other schools;
- fail to attract high quality teachers into posts because the school is seen to be failing;
- receive negative Ofsted reports;
- achieve low test and examination results;
- use suspensions and exclusions too frequently in their attempt to manage behaviour;
- lose valuable members of staff, who leave to work in successful schools.

Teachers will:

- need time away from school with stress-related illness;
- stagger on for years, experiencing little job satisfaction and feeling personally unfulfilled;
- create a negative effect on school achievement;
- alienate pupils who will begin to associate school with failure;
- intimidate timid pupils, who may feel threatened by the lack of discipline and take time off school;
- be responsible for low school-attendance figures;
- affect the quality of learning, so that most pupils underachieve;
- produce disruptive pupils who proceed to model bad behaviour throughout the school, affecting the behaviour of the rest of the pupils;
- confirm the belief of those parents whose own school experience was negative that school is, indeed, a waste of time.

Parents will:

- observe displays of unacceptable behaviour and gain a poor impression of the school;
- become disillusioned with the school and fail to communicate and co-operate;
- be concerned about the low standard of education achieved in the school;
- withdraw their children from the school;
- recommend other parents do not send their children to the school.

Pupils will:

- become unhappy and perhaps fearful;
- not reach their full potential;

- begin to 'hate' school;
- fail to attend school regularly;
- become bored, disillusioned and disruptive.

If schools are to succeed, it is vital that all staff are equipped with the skills to manage the challenge to their authority, and schools must make this possible by establishing a supportive structure and ethos.

'It was never like this in my day,' says Grandad

It is not simply nostalgia that dictates the opinion that behaviour in schools is deteriorating. Research exists to confirm it as fact:

- A recent study, 'Time Trends in Adolescent Mental Health' Collishaw *et al.* (2004), reported that the mental health of teenagers has declined sharply in the last 25 years, and the chance that 15-year-olds will have behavioural problems has more than doubled.
- In 2001, the Ofsted Annual Report concluded that one in twelve secondary schools and one in fifty primary schools experiences unsatisfactory behaviour which seriously affects the school.
- The National Union of Teachers revealed that more than 80 per cent of teachers felt that behaviour had deteriorated during their time in teaching.
- The national children's mental health charity Young Minds believes that up to 40 per cent of young people in inner-city areas now present emotional and behavioural problems.

Many of these troubled children are in our schools, and of course their problems will have an impact on their ability to learn, and on how they choose to behave. Other contributory factors include poor early family attachment, domestic violence and family break-up — all of which leave children feeling lonely, confused, sad and angry. They may choose to act out their anger in the classroom.

So, investigations prove that behaviour in schools has indeed declined. We need to take a closer look at why this has occurred.

Who is responsible?

There is undoubtedly no single cause for the perceived decline in standards of behaviour in schools, and there is much speculation about who or what is responsible. The finger of blame cannot be pointed in any one direction. The following have all at various times and for various reasons been in the firing line. Let's start at the top.

The Department for Education and Skills

The DfES has been accused of providing insufficient funding for education, resulting in:

- overlarge classes;
- inadequate resources;

"Well I blame the DfES, the LEA, the headteachers, the parents, computer games and fizzy drinks"

- cramped and dingy school accommodation which is inadequate for the needs of pupils and staff;
- inconsistent teaching assistant (TA) support;
- inadequate school meals, lacking in nutrition;
- a National Curriculum that may be too inflexible and therefore inappropriate for some pupils;
- the existing policy to include most pupils with SEN in mainstream schools, which may be unrealistic in the case of those exhibiting highly dysfunctional behaviour;
- the current emphasis on academic success, which may cause a sense of failure and demotivation for low achievers or the less able;
- the current programme of training for student teachers, which may be inadequate regarding the management of behaviour.

Local education authorities

Local education authorities (LEAs) have been seen as lacking in:

- fair distribution of funding to schools;
- the provision of sufficient well-trained professionals (educational psychologists, behaviour support services, child psychiatrists, family therapists and counsellors);
- regular training for schools in the management of behaviour;
- counselling provision in schools for pupils and their families when necessary;
- provision for pupils excluded from school.

Schools

Schools have been accused of contributing to the problem through:

- inadequate behaviour policies;
- school organisations that do not reflect the behaviour policy;
- lack of co-operation with LEAs;
- inadequate support and training for all staff in behaviour management;
- inadequate training for teachers in using TA support to help manage behaviour in classrooms;
- inadequate training for teachers currently working with pupils already identified with particular special needs that will affect their behaviour;
- not making staff such as lunchtime supervisors, TAs, supply teachers, bus drivers and learning mentors aware of the situation of particular pupils;
- inadequate induction and support for non-qualified teachers (NQTs);
- allowing on-site vending machines that encourage the consumption of fizzy drinks and additive-rich junk foods, which may cause hyperactivity;
- neglecting to educate children about the importance of a healthy lifestyle;
- failing to create a positive learning environment.

Parents

Perhaps the largest share of blame is attached to the parents of badly behaved children. They have been charged with failing to:

- provide adequate care and protection for their children;
- ensure their children eat breakfast, and have a generally healthy diet and adequate sleep;
- provide a quiet place for homework;
- support the school in actions taken to curb difficult behaviour;
- supply their children with equipment needed for school;
- act as effective role models and establish a culture in the home in which aggression, disrespect for others, manipulation and swearing are unacceptable;
- protect their children from anxiety when home circumstances are difficult.

Food for thought

In 2005, the Child Behavioural Index Study revealed that 70 per cent of children in the UK were badly behaved, and much of the blame was placed with parents. The three main issues were:
- poor diet;
- children allowed to spend too much time watching TV and playing computer games;
- too little discipline in the home.

Outside influences

Other factors identified as having a possible negative influence on pupil behaviour include:

- exposure to unsuitable TV programmes or films;
- violent computer games;
- peer-group pressure;
- mental health or other medical problems;
- the availability of alcohol and drugs.

Pupils

The question of pupil responsibility is an interesting and delicate one. Whilst behaviour is undoubtedly influenced by any number of external agencies – such as the home, the school and the DfES – the principle of the responsibility of individuals for their own behaviour is an important one that is often lost in the debate. Of course, it is our responsibility to ensure that we create, by all means possible, conditions that do not encourage dysfunctional behaviour, and that we do all we can to provide a positive influence. Nevertheless, the responsibility for behaviour lies with the pupil. There are some pupils who are diagnosed with an emotional, mental or genetic disorder (see Chapter 2) and who cannot always be made accountable for their actions; they may, indeed, be misplaced in a mainstream school. The majority of pupils, however, are choosing, for whatever reason, to break rules or to behave disrespectfully to others.

Food for thought

The Serenity Prayer
God grant me the serenity
To accept the things I cannot change,
The courage to change the things I can,
And the wisdom to know the difference.

Anon.

Teachers

Arguably the most important factor in the management of behaviour in schools is teachers themselves. Teachers have very little control over most of the factors listed above (although some of them may be within their sphere of influence), but what is under the teacher's control is the teaching. As we all must know from our own childhood school experiences, teachers have the power to influence their pupils for good or ill.

What can teachers do?

Teachers can do what most of them are doing already – which is a very good job, and the best they can. The Ofsted report *Managing Challenging Behaviour* confirms this view:

> The behaviour of the very large majority of pupils and students remains satisfactory or better. Most schools and settings are successful at managing behaviour and creating an environment in which learners feel valued, cared for and safe.

However, most teachers, even those who are very effective and skilled in the task of managing behaviour, will agree there is always something new to learn. This book aims to provide ideas that will further enhance the skills of accomplished teachers, and offers starting points for those who are less experienced or are struggling.

Some teachers may find it difficult to admit they have a problem, choosing to blame the school, the pupils, the environment or the subject they teach. They may even be aware that in the hands of other teachers their nightmare classes are well behaved and on task most of the time – but are choosing to ignore it. It is, perhaps, an uncomfortable fact that some teachers need more support and training than others to get them started. But simply requiring more help in the early stages does not necessarily mean there is a fundamental problem, nor does it mean that higher levels of competence cannot be achieved. Some people need a lot more practice than others before passing their driving test, but go on to become competent, confident drivers.

Take a look at this widely used four-stage model of learning, as related to learning the skill of managing behaviour.

Stage 1: Unconscious incompetence

This is the stage when you are trying to teach an unruly, uncooperative class and have no idea about preventive measures, effective differentiation, and strategies, so you accept the situation. You think, 'Oh well, this is how it is.' You have no idea what your options are. The class are making little progress, and you do not take any personal responsibility. Things couldn't be worse! You don't know that you don't know.

The role of the effective school

The senior management team (SMT) have in place an induction programme that ensures all new staff are familiar with the school behaviour policy, and also have opportunities to observe other teachers, before they take up their teaching or TA role. The monitoring system in the school will have identified which teachers are in need of extra support, and will offer it without being asked. A good school is aware of the issues and is prepared to take early action. It is proactive.

Stage 2: Conscious incompetence

This is a healthy stage, when you begin to realise your inadequacies, accept the class are underachieving and behaving badly, and look for support. Things can only get better! You know that you don't know.

The role of the effective school

The school creates an ethos that encourages any members of staff who feel they have problems to discuss them freely, without shame. The school will have procedures in place to support teachers who need it. This may involve providing:

- ⊙ additional TA help;
- ⊙ extra training courses;
- ⊙ useful behaviour management literature;
- ⊙ opportunities to observe other teachers at work;
- ⊙ a mentor.

The school will monitor the progress of the teacher and provide additional help, if needed. This may involve employing a consultant to observe the teacher and give individual feedback. The teacher will be respected by the school as they have overcome the first hurdle and had the courage to ask for support. A good school will certainly listen, and will provide what is needed. Schools need effective teachers.

Stage 3: Conscious competence

Things are getting better! You realise that you need to adjust your seating plan, to differentiate your lessons to make them interesting to all, and to use some strategies to manage behaviour. You also have learned how to avoid confrontation, but you can deal with conflict, should it arise. The class are making progress. You have gained confidence. You know that you know.

The role of the effective school

The school continues to provide regular training and updates to all staff, and reviews the behaviour policy with them annually. There is a system in place for monitoring behaviour in school, to raise awareness of possible improvements that might be needed. A good school knows it is essential to have this structure in place as it helps staff to be more confident, secure in the fact they know exactly what to do whenever a situation arises.

Stage 4: Unconscious competence

Things couldn't be better! You have arrived. You just get on with the job, dealing effectively with behaviour. Strategies are used automatically, and you have built up a good relationship with the pupils in which they respect you for who you are. But you never sit back and think there's nothing more to learn. You continue to attend training courses, and read up on the latest projects and initiatives. You don't know that you know.

"Thank you for providing me with this opportunity to learn, Natasha!"

The role of the effective school

The school has and shows respect and appreciation for their teachers who work hard at maintaining this level of efficiency. They are too valuable to lose, so the school ensures that provision for the staff, including the working environment, is comfortable, that staff have opportunities to air their views – and that they are listened to. A happy staff is not a continually changing one.

It can never be assumed that teachers new to the profession will be at Stage 1. I have observed NQTs who from Day 1 seem to be operating at the unconsciously competent level. Lucky them. Most teachers, however, learn on the job and will experience all four stages. We need to remember that the most challenging pupils offer us more learning opportunities than the well behaved, who just gobble up the curriculum and pass exams without a murmur. Indeed, we need to see challenging behaviour for what it is: a challenge and not a problem.

Now that we have made a reality check on deteriorating behaviour and the teacher's position, the next chapter will identify the types of behaviour encountered and outline the support that should be available to schools.

Chapter 2
What is challenging behaviour?

Research carried out by the University of Birmingham in 2005 identified the two most challenging types of behaviour, and there is widespread agreement on these. The first is violent behaviour such as biting, kicking, throwing furniture and assault; the second is verbal aggression such as streams of abuse, temper tantrums, refusal to work and invasion of others' personal space. However, the Ofsted report *Managing Challenging Behaviour* (2005) found that the most common form of poor behaviour is 'persistent low-level disruption' of lessons that wears down staff and interrupts learning. Extreme acts of violence remain very rare and are carried out by a small proportion of pupils.

The Ofsted report also found that 'lack of definition about what constitutes challenging behaviour makes it difficult to gauge the full extent of it'. The type of challenging behaviour experienced by teachers, of course, will vary according to the age of pupils and the subjects being taught. For example, a science teacher with a Year 9 class may experience problems with pupils and Bunsen burners, whilst a Reception teacher is more likely to encounter pupils with tantrums which involve screaming fits and hitting other children.

Types of low-level disruption

The behaviours detailed on the checklist on page 18 represent the 'persistent low-level disruption' described in the report. Many of these negative behaviours may be very familiar to you, but it is important to be aware, not only of the behaviour you don't want, but also of the behaviour you do want. This will boost your confidence in your interactions with disruptive pupils. You may find it a useful exercise to check which behaviours you encounter, and to identify the target behaviour in each case.

Types of high-level disruption

As well as the low-level type of disruption, more serious incidents may occur. Over the last few years, many teachers have experienced pupils:

- tearing up their own or other pupils' work;
- throwing articles around the classroom;
- making faces at the class from outside the room, in the corridor;
- leaving the class or school premises without permission;
- throwing objects out of the window at pupils passing by;
- throwing a computer (yes, a computer) out of the window;
- hiding in cupboards or under tables and refusing to come out;
- swearing at the teacher or TA;
- staring into the classroom to distract the pupils there, and refusing to come into the class or move away;

"A science teacher with a Year 9 class may experience problems with pupils and Bunsen burners."

Behaviour checklist

Negative behaviour	Target behaviour
Talking out of turn	To talk only at appropriate times, e.g. when doing group work
Shouting out in class	To put hands up and wait to be asked for a contribution
Verbally abusing another pupil	
Deliberately avoiding work	
Being late for school or lessons	
Physically abusing another pupil	
Walking about in class inappropriately	
Failing to bring PE kit or other equipment	
Leaving the class without permission	
Fidgetting or lolling about in class	
Entering the room noisily	
Failing to do homework	
Making deliberate noise	
Verbally abusing the teacher or TA	
Mimicking the teacher or TA	
Refusing to work	
Using a mobile phone in class	
Arguing with the teacher or TA	
Using a personal CD player in class	
Going on to inappropriate Internet sites	

- throwing small objects at the teacher when their back is turned;
- making personal or sexual comments about the teacher's appearance;
- refusing to leave the room when asked;
- dropping to the floor and lying very still;
- destroying school property or that of another pupil;
- physically abusing the teacher or TA.

Before you head for the nearest Careers Advice Centre in order to see what jobs, other than teaching, are available, you should know that some of the more extreme behaviours were reported by teachers in special schools. These teachers will have developed skills in dealing with highly dysfunctional behaviour, and will have received extra training and support to help them cope. However, we are talking mainstream for many behaviours recorded here. Scary, isn't it?

Troubled or troublesome?

Before we begin to consider the question of behaviour management, we need to be aware that there are pupils in our schools who, for one reason or another, will not respond to skilled teaching. The Office for National Statistics (ONS) report that 10 per cent of children have mental health disorders which are deep rooted and profound, and which will affect their ability to make relationships and learn. A senior educational psychologist colleague who worked for many years with severely disruptive pupils confirmed these findings at grass-roots level. He perceived pupils with challenging behaviour as fitting into one of two categories: the **troubled** and the **troublesome**. He agreed with the findings of the ONS, and estimated that 10 per cent of pupils were troubled and therefore not open to responding to basic, everyday behaviour strategies. The government drive towards including the vast majority of pupils in mainstream schools means that many of these pupils, who previously would have attended special schools or units, are in mainstream education. The remaining 90 per cent of pupils he considered to be potentially troublesome, given the chance.

The Department for Education and Employment, some years ago, drew our attention to the importance of recognising troublesome, as opposed to troubled, behaviour. This is what they had to say:

> Emotional and behavioural difficulties lie on the continuum between behaviour that challenges teachers but is within normal, albeit unacceptable bounds, and that which is indicative of serious mental illness. The distinction between normal but stressed behaviour, emotional and behavioural difficulties, and behaviour arising from mental illness is important because each needs to be treated differently.
>
> Definition of EBD, DfEE (1994)

It is important that pupils from the troubled category have their particular problems recognised. Don't make the assumption that they will already have been identified. Some pupils have spent years in schools where they have been labelled as highly disruptive, when the truth is that they are highly troubled. These pupils need some kind of professional help which it is beyond the capacity of the school to provide. It may be that their behaviour reflects extreme emotional difficulties resulting from traumatic life experiences such as physical, sexual or emotional abuse. On the other hand, disorders such as Attention Deficit Hyperactivity Disorder (ADHD), Attention Deficit Disorder (ADD) or Autistic Spectrum Disorders (ASD) – which includes pupils with Asperger Syndrome – may be responsible. Depression, anxiety, obsessive-compulsive disorder or some kind of conduct disorder may also be causes. These disorders need to be understood. ADHD and Asperger Syndrome are probably the most prevalent amongst pupils with behaviour problems whom we encounter in schools. The Ofsted report draws exactly the same distinction. It acknowledges the (increased) presence of 'pupils displaying behaviour related to medical needs' and suggests that 'strategies to manage these pupils will differ from those in use with the majority'.

Food for thought

Stephen Bradshaw, executive director of Priory Education Services, which specialise in the education of pupils with Asperger Syndrome, gives a powerful indication of problems which may arise because of lack of identification:

This lack of diagnosis can go on for years, with devastating consequences when children try to take their own lives, because they can't cope with being different any longer. In later years, many children with AS are arrested and imprisoned as their behaviour is considered anti-social. Correct diagnosis and a wider awareness of AS is therefore vital.

S. Bradshaw (2004)

Identifying the troubled

So teachers need to be ever vigilant. They need to know that troubled pupils cannot respond to the regular day-to-day strategies. When teachers observe behaviours which are extreme or unusual in any way, they need to keep a daily record of incidents and report these to the SENCo. If, following advice from the SENCo, it is decided that the pupil's behaviour indicates they have SEN, they need to be placed at School Action on the school's SEN profile. Additional support and strategies must be introduced and an individual behaviour plan prepared. If the pupil fails to respond to the targets set on the plan, the SENCo will recommend to the LEA that the pupil receives additional, external support and be placed at School Action Plus. Enter the LEA.

The role of the LEA

Decisions will be made by the LEA, together with the parents and school, regarding the type of support the pupil requires, and it may not be possible to offer this within a mainstream establishment. However, most pupils, given extra support, are able to cope, but their teachers will also need support and extra training. The support offered may include the allocation of a TA. The progress of the pupil will be monitored by an educational psychologist or a member of the LEA Behaviour Support Service. A particular intervention programme may be recommended. Counselling, anger management classes and other forms of therapeutic intervention may be available. If pupils fails to make progress at this stage, the LEA, following a statutory assessment, may award a statement to guarantee the funding and support required to maintain the pupil in school. At some stage, the decision may involve placing the pupil in a special school or unit where their needs may be better catered for. The services of the Health Authority are usually sought in the identification of a particular disorder and appropriate drugs may be prescribed.

> Pupils with SEN that require 'school action' or 'school action plus' or those who have a statement of SEN form at least one third of pupils identified as having behavioural difficulties in the secondary schools visited. In primary schools few of those identified have a statement for ESBD but one third require 'school action' or 'school action plus'.
>
> Ofsted (2005)

The strategies used for troubled pupils should be different from those used on a day-to-day basis with the remainder of the class. Schools will usually explore all possible channels in their effort to maintain pupils in school, before resorting to the ultimate sanction: permanent exclusion. The effects of this action on already troubled pupils can be devastating. For more information on this, see Charlie Cooper's *Understanding School Exclusion* (2002).

Understanding the troublesome

However, it is the troublesome – those who create challenging behaviour from choice and who are not much influenced by additional internal factors – who are the main focus of this book.

The Ofsted report (pp. 8–9) provides some interesting information regarding the characteristics of learners showing challenging behaviour. Here is a summary of the findings:

- ◐ Boys are more likely than girls to be both physically and verbally abusive.
- ◐ Many pupils with the most challenging behaviour have joined at times other than the usual point of admission.
- ◐ Many pupils showing challenging behaviour in early years settings, mainstream schools and PRUs are from troubled families or are in public care.
- ◐ Irregular attendance is an issue for large numbers of pupils with challenging behaviour, which leads to breaks in learning and in the development of positive relationships with staff and peers.
- ◐ In most primary schools, only a small proportion of pupils with challenging behaviour are from minority ethnic groups. The proportion is higher in secondary schools and PRUs, and in some of special schools in inner city areas.

○ A significant proportion of pupils with challenging behaviour have poor language and social skills and limited concentration spans. Two thirds of pupils who have been excluded from school have reading ages two or three years below their chronological age, and struggle to read and comprehend material in lessons. They also have limited writing skills.

So, it is possible to identify some general characteristics of troublesome pupils, and it is useful to have at least some insight into why Jamie may choose to refuse to work, and spits at Chantelle in the playground. However, it is vital that, whatever the circumstances surrounding the challenging behaviour, teachers do not lower their expectations. It is important not to patronise Jamie by accepting his challenging behaviour, just because his father is an alcoholic and his mother is in prison. Have compassion for the situation, yes, but set about establishing a relationship with the child that helps him to feel accepted and cared for. That he can 'do it'. That he is as important as the rest of the class. That he is not a hopeless victim. That you believe in him. And yes, some of us face greater challenges in life than others, but feeling sorry for Jamie will simply confirm in his own mind that indeed he is a hopeless case. I think that probably the greatest gift a teacher can impart to any pupil is to help them believe they are worthwhile.

Having distinguished between the troubled and the troublesome, we shall now turn to look at ways in which the school can create a positive environment that is conducive to good behaviour.

A teacher affects eternity: he can never tell where his influence stops.

Henry Brooks Adams

Chapter 3
Creating a positive learning environment

A successful school is one that is able to create a positive learning environment, one that limits the possibility of disruptive behaviour occurring in the first place. In addition, this school will ensure that all staff are well trained, that a consistent approach is taken towards the management of behaviour, and that clear guidelines have been established to enable staff to deal with any incident that may confront them. In other words, a successful school is proactive. The model below represents the approach taken by positive schools.

A model of behaviour management
The positive model

Dealing with confrontation — Troubleshooting

Managing behaviour with classroom strategies — Management

Creating a positive learning environment — Prevention

The establishment of a positive school environment in the lowest layer will directly influence the second layer, since such an environment means the incidence of disruptive behaviour in classrooms is less likely. So fewer challenges will take place in the classroom, and the role of teachers (that is, to teach) will be made easier. In the top layer, the occurrence of incidents will be rare; work put in on the lower layers reduces the possibility of bad behaviour occurring and the consequent need to deal with it.

Let's see what happens in a highly dysfunctional school.

The negative model

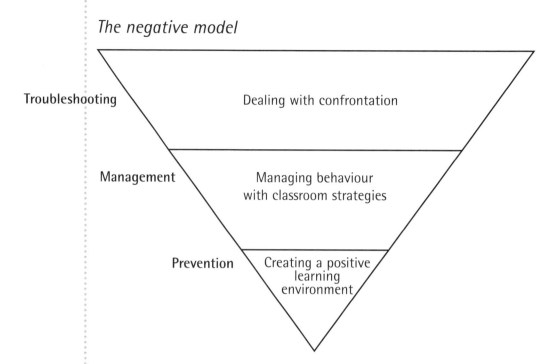

This model reflects what happens in a school which has failed to create the circumstances necessary for the successful management of behaviour. The school has become reactive because the environment essential to promote learning and good behaviour has not been established, and the consequent high levels of disruptive behaviour are not managed effectively by the staff. The majority of the school's effort is directed at the top layer, managing incidents; they have taken a negative reactive approach. They get involved after things have gone wrong. The ever-escalating level of disruption in these schools will have grave consequences for the standards of education achieved. In their report *Managing Challenging Behaviour* (2005), Ofsted analyse the reasons for and consequences of the negative approach, and these are summarised below:

- In some schools, policies are overcomplex, do not promote consistency of expectation, or do not emphasise the encouragement of good behaviour. When there are inconsistencies, those who have more difficulty in moderating their own behaviour are unclear about boundaries.

- A negative emphasis in behaviour policies often results in a focus on dealing with problems after they have occurred.

- In a small proportion of schools, exclusion is used as a way of enabling teachers to cope more effectively with difficult behaviour. This does not necessarily enhance teachers' confidence and ability to manage poor behaviour.

- In many schools visited, pupils' needs are identified too late and there is insufficient analysis of patterns of behaviour. In these schools there is usually a crisis that leads to belated action.

- In all the schools where the curriculum is limited and differentiation is lacking, there is a high level of poor behaviour as pupils' interest, motivation and involvement decline.

○ In a small proportion of primary schools, the curriculum is not differentiated appropriately for some pupils.

○ Some schools fail to realise the importance of the link between behaviour and the curriculum.

○ In some schools, difficulties in recruiting staff have adversely affected the range of courses offered.

○ Late starts to lessons, disorganised classrooms, low expectations and unsuitable tasks allow inappropriate behaviour to flourish.

○ Pupils often act badly when staff show a lack of respect or interest in them.

○ Deteriorating behaviour goes hand-in-hand with a decline in the quality of teaching. Among the factors that influence this are: changes of staff, lack of consistency of expectation, failure to plan lessons satisfactorily to meet wide ranges of need, and lack of variety of strategies to engage pupils in learning.

So, how do schools create a positive school environment?

Creating a positive learning environment
What should be in place?
The Ofsted report provides information on effective action to manage and improve behaviour. This is guidance based on their observation of schools which have established a positive working environment. Set out below are the key findings from the Ofted report. The arrow bullet points provide examples of ways in which one particular school – Blakehall Heath Junior School – has successfully established this kind of environment.

Policies on behaviour
Most of the schools and colleges visited have behaviour policies which set out expectations clearly.

○ There is a well-defined, democratically produced behaviour policy which is reviewed annually by the whole staff.

○ All pupils sign a contract to say that they understand and agree to the school rules.

○ Clear and simple school rules are displayed in all classrooms, and there are notices around school with polite reminders about what is expected.

○ Children are sent to the head only under exceptional circumstances. A child sent to the head will be accompanied by a TA or responsible pupil to ensure the head is available; if not, they will accompany the pupil back to the class. This ensures the headteacher sanction is not abused and is seen as serious.

Ethos
A school's ethos provides the context within which children feel secure, know they are valued as individuals, are safe from emotional and physical harm, and are able to discuss their interests and voice their fears in a supportive atmosphere.

○ The school follows a programme of accelerated learning.

○ A healthy choice of food is available for school lunches and break times.

○ Pupils are allowed free access to drinking water and are encouraged to eat fresh fruit.

○ There is a breakfast club for pupils who arive at school not having had breakfast. Such pupils would otherwise often find it difficult to concentrate and be more likely to misbehave.

○ Strong links are made with all possible support: health and social services, the LEA, parents, education welfare officers, behaviour support services and so on.

The development of a school's ethos falls to the senior management, but its growth and maintenance depends on the involvement of the whole staff.

○ The staff act as positive role models. They care about their pupils and demonstrate this.

Inspection and research continually reaffirm the importance of consistency in the way staff themselves behave and act, in and around the school. This helps boys, particularly, to behave better and achieve more.

○ The school seeks out information regarding new behaviour initiatives and passes this information on to the staff.

Support for staff

Most of the schools visited had policies and procedures for staff induction.

The most difficult behaviour is almost always managed well in schools with the following attributes:
- *Strong senior managers give clear direction and reassuring support for staff. These effective leaders monitor the management of behaviour.*
- *The regular presence of senior managers around school is seen by teachers as important in developing a sense of calm and order and enabling the managers to understand the difficulties with behaviour that teachers face.*
- *Regular opportunities are organised so that staff discuss behaviour issues and have opportunities to learn from colleagues and observe good practice.*
- *A strong staff team is created in which the emphasis is on mutual support.*
- *Good quality written guidance – for example, in staff handbooks – helps new staff to come to terms quickly with the standards and expectations of the school.*

○ Lunch breaks are short and well supervised so pupils do not become bored and restless. The shorter lunch breaks enable lunchtime supervisors to be present 10 minutes before and after their time in contact with pupils, allowing opportunity to discuss any problems they may have experienced.

- There is ample TA support; TAs are well managed and know how to support teachers effectively with the management of behaviour.
- Social activities are arranged regularly for all staff.

Staff training

Regular training that links classroom practice to an understanding of how children develop socially and emotionally is central to the effective understanding and management of behaviour.

- There are regular training sessions for all staff, including TAs.
- There is training on ways in which TAs may support teachers with the management of behaviour.
- Lunchtime supervisors are well trained.
- There is a good supply of books on the management of behaviour available for all staff.

Tracking and analysing behaviour

Some of the schools carry out detailed tracking of learning and behaviour, identify pupils' needs and quickly take action.

- As directed by the behaviour policy, the staff keep incident records of daily problems and inform the behaviour co-ordinator of recurring issues. The behaviour co-ordinator discusses the best way forward, for example discussions with pupils, with parents, or with the headteacher. Pupils and parents are aware of this procedure because it is outlined in the behaviour policy.

Adaptation of the curriculum

An appropriate curriculum is offered in all the early years settings visited, in almost all of the primary, special schools and PRUs and in about three quarters of secondary schools.

The majority of schools recognise the importance of using the curriculum flexibly to capture pupils' interests.

Out-of-hours activities

Some of the schools, in particular secondary schools, have found that a good range of additional activities increases interest and better engages poorly behaved pupils.

- Staff provide varied extra-curricular activities which demonstrate their genuine interest in the children's welfare and provide additional learning opportunities. They also allow staff to relate to pupils in a more social context.
- The school football team acts as an incentive to pupils. It provides opportunities for some pupils to experience success and the rest to feel proud and supportive of their school. It provides a further bond with the staff.

Well-focused pastoral support and guidance

Support and guidance tend to be good in schools where there is a strong sense of community and the staff regularly celebrate pupils' successes. The most effective pastoral support systems are those in which there is careful and regular tracking of pupils' learning and behaviour.

- The employment of a learning mentor in the school has proved invaluable, as they are able to offer support to teachers by supporting challenging pupils in class, by withdrawing pupils when appropriate to enable them to calm down, and by listening to pupils who may be upset.
- The learning mentor visits parents at home to discuss behaviour issues.
- The learning mentor works with small groups of pupils on behaviour management, and regularly monitors pupils whose behaviour is or has been an issue.
- The learning mentor is available to act as counsellor/friend to pupils who may need to discuss some problems and may act as a go-between for pupil, parent and teacher.

Rewards and celebration

Schools which support pupils well are quick to acknowledge and celebrate pupils' achievement and reward systems are applied consistently.

- The school has adapted the You Can Do It project (Michael Barnard) and the reward system is linked to four foundation behaviours: confidence, persistence, getting on with others and being well organised. Pupils are rewarded for showing the 'four foundation behaviours', not only for good work and behaviour.

Responsibilities

In many of the schools and units pupils are encouraged to take responsibility for every aspect of school life.

- Pupils who do present challenging behaviour are requested to give consideration to the situation and fill in 'rethink' sheets. These will identify the trigger for the unacceptable behaviour and also teach them acceptable options to replace the type of behaviour which comes naturally to them when dealing with conflict.

In these schools teachers listen to pupils and involve them in whole-school decisions, for example, through the school council.

- There is a school council where the members may discuss behaviour problems and possible solutions.

Often they develop school and class rules and work alongside staff in setting and reviewing their own targets.

'Circle time' is well used in many primary schools and some of the secondary schools to promote school rules and develop strategies to enable pupils to take responsibility.

Some of the schools have a 'buddy' or peer mentoring systems which support pupils with the most challenging behaviour well.

◐ The school runs a buddies system whereby certain pupils may be allocated a buddy (a responsible, trained pupil) who meets them regularly to see how they are getting on and to act as a support.

Some of the secondary schools successfully use 'restorative justice' to help pupils take responsibility for their own behaviour.

Good involvement of parents and carers

Links with parents are most successful when parents are seen as partners rather than being blamed for the poor behaviour of their children.

Parents welcome news of their children's successes as well as being informed of unacceptable behaviour.

◐ Parents are encouraged to participate in school. An outline of the school behaviour policy is included in the school prospectus, and parents are asked to sign a home–school agreement to say that they agree to the school rules and will support the school in its effort to manage the behaviour of their child.

◐ The school has an open door policy, and parents may come and talk with staff at the beginning and end of each day.

◐ Parents are involved with the administration of the rethink sheets, and may send messages to school in the homework diaries if there are any concerns.

A welcoming environment

The quality of the learning environment has a significant impact on the behaviour of pupils and students; it should not be underestimated.

◐ The school's physical environment has been made attractive, by the introduction of playground games, picnic benches and seating.

◐ There is attractively presented comfortable seating in the reception area to welcome visitors to the school, who are given a friendly greeting by the secretary on arrival. Photo albums of the school children participating in various activities are available for visitors to look at.

◐ Pupils' work is attractively displayed in corridors as well as classrooms.

◐ There is an attractive, welcoming staff room.

◐ The environment is pleasant and welcoming, due to the care taken by the cleaning staff.

◐ There are pleasant toilet facilities for both staff and pupils.

Many thanks to Ofsted and Blakenall Heath Junior School for the suggestions made here to support schools in establishing an environment conducive to positive behaviour and learning.

The first step in establishing a positive learning environment is to analyse the ways in which the school currently provides for this. The SMT could invite all staff to participate in the analysis, and to identify any actions required. You may find it helpful to use the checklist on pages 31 and 32, which provides a framework for analysis, based on the areas listed above from the Ofsted report.

The checklist could either be filled in by individual members of staff or it could be used to stimulate discussion, with a scribe recording responses to the points raised.

Following the exercise, you may find you need to prepare an action plan to modify, introduce or curtail certain activities in the school. The exercise will also provide a clear idea of the staff perception of the support available to them, and indicate whether further support should be provided.

Behaviour policy • Is this clear to all and reviewed annually? • Do rewards match the needs of the pupils? • Are sanctions applied consistently throughout the school, and are they working?	
Ethos • Do pupils feel secure? • Do they know they are valued as individuals? • Are they safe from physical and emotional harm? • Are they able to discuss their interests and voice their fears?	
Support for all staff, including teachers, TAs and lunchtime supervisors • What support in the management of behaviour is currently available to you from the SMT? • Is this adequate? If not, what type of support you would like to see in place?	
Staff training • What training have you received on the management of behaviour since you joined this school? • Is this adequate? If not, what additional training would be useful?	
Tracking and analysing behaviour • How is behaviour monitored in this school? • What are the results of these investigations? • How is this information fed back to you? • What action have you observed being taken as a result of findings?	

Out-of-hours activities • What existing extra-curricular activities take place in the school? • Do you see these as a valuable contribution to the school in relation to behaviour issues? Why / Why not? • Would you be willing to make a contribution in this area?	
Rewards and celebration • Does the school reward and celebrate the pupils (and staff)? • If so, how is this achieved? • Do you feel it is adequate? If not, what more could be done?	
Good involvement of parents and carers • What is the existing involvement of parents and carers? • Do you feel this is adequate? If not, in what ways could parents and carers become more involved?	
Responsibilities • What opportunities are there for pupils to take some sort of responsibility in school? • Are these adequate? If not, what other opportunities could be provided? • Does the school sufficiently involve pupils in supporting their peers who are disruptive? • In what ways does the school encourage pupils to take responsibility for their own behaviour?	
A welcoming environment • Is the physical environment attractive for both pupils and staff? • Are there areas that could be improved? If so, how? • Are visitors to the school made to feel welcome?	

Chapter 4
Managing behaviour with classroom strategies

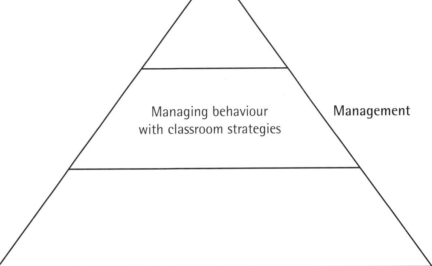

Now we arrive at the second layer of the model, managing for good behaviour in the classroom. If the school has put in the necessary work to create a purposeful and positive environment, the classroom management role becomes much easier. By taking care over preparation and employing a range of strategies to manage their relationship with pupils, the teacher can build on the positive foundations. Of course, some teachers are faced with shaky foundations; whilst this is not ideal, the approach described in this chapter will still be of use to them.

Before we consider strategies, however, let's take a step back.

Who you are is more important than what you do

In general, a teacher's success in managing behaviour depends much more on who they are, their personality and their communication skills, than on what they actually do. If you are genuinely interested in pupils and have an interest and, better still, a passion for teaching, and are willing to learn from the pupils who are sitting in front of you, then you will experience few problems with behaviour that challenges teaching.

Of course, underlying who you are as a teacher are your reasons and motivation for doing this most challenging of jobs. It is not within the scope of this book to provide careers guidance; this is simply to note that a genuine commitment to education and to the children you teach is a prerequisite for real success. When pupils know they are liked and respected, they in turn will like and respect their teachers, and this will be reflected in their behaviour. This is reflected in the following poem.

The Earth Awaits Us

He was a man
Down to earth
Free and alone
Not lonely
Independent
Always ready for us.

He was my teacher
He wasn't old.
He died in school
And nobody saved him.

He was a man I will always
Remember.
Kind and clever.
For good homework he would draw
In our exercise books
Little pictures to please us.

At break time in the classroom
He smoked his pipe at his desk.
At Christmas I gave him a tin of
Old Holborn.

That year we won the cups
For football and netball.
After the match we went to his
house.
'The best teams in the country',
he told us.

He raised money for Ethiopia,
roller skating.
Our class broke the record.
Our pictures were in the paper
The only one I've got of him.

He loved his family and his garden
Weekends he dug the earth.
He talked to us about his flowers
And shared memories of places.

One day he drew in a circle
On the blackboard
A dancer turning on a dais
To music from Coppelia.
We'd been by coach to see the
matinee.
After he'd died we left the picture
On the board for days.
He died in the school play dancing.
Laughing and dancing.

We planted a tree in the earth
In the school field where we can
see it.
So he would always be part of our
lives.
We will always remember him.

They buried him in the earth
By the old churchyard.
The earth is free and alone
Not lonely.
Independent.
Always ready for us.

Sophie Benzing, aged 13, winner of
the *Observer* National Poetry
Competition, 1997

Only the brave should teach. Only those who love the young should teach. Teaching is a vocation. It is as sacred as priesthood; as innate a desire, as inescapable as the genius that compels a great artist. If he has not the concern for humanity, the love of living creatures, the vision of the priest and the artist, he must not teach.
Pearl S. Buck

What is certain is that all teachers will be faced with challenging behaviour at some time. Skilled management will usually ensure the challenge does not escalate into chaos. What does skilled management entail? There are three main areas that teachers and TAs need to consider:

- ❍ being prepared;
- ❍ using strategies to manage the day-to-day relationship with pupils;
- ❍ dealing with conflict.

The first two points relate to the middle layer of our model, and we shall consider these in the rest of this chapter. The third point is what happens in the top layer, and will be dealt with in Chapter 5.

But first, bearing in mind the principle that prevention is always better than cure, we shall consider how preparation can minimise the possible incidence of disruption in the classroom.

Preparation

Here are some measures that will help to ensure your classroom is a place conducive to good behaviour.

The classroom

Take care with the appearance of the classroom. Ask yourself 'Is this a pleasant and comfortable working environment and, if not, is there something I can do to improve it?'

Ensure the temperature, lighting and classroom furniture are suitable. Pupils' physical needs are paramount. Being too hot, too cold or uncomfortable will lead to off-task behaviour.

Lesson planning

Plan lessons in advance. When lessons haven't been planned properly and targets are not set or clarified, this can result in confusion and a lack of interest.

Be aware of different learning styles and differentiate accordingly. If you are not too sure about the significance of learning styles, it will be helpful to read up on it. Alistair Smith's *Accelerated Learning in the Classroom* (1996) would be a good start. Pupils learn much better and are less likely to become bored and off-task if you take account of different learning styles.

Keep the lesson pace brisk. Include different activities. Keep strict time boundaries.

Involve TAs in the lesson plans. For TAs to be effective, they need to know in advance what the lesson content will be. This information will help their confidence in managing pupils and they are less likely to encounter the gibe 'You're not a teacher. You can't tell me what to do!'

Clarify the role of the TA in advance regarding the management of behaviour. This is important. See page 37 for more.

Organisation

Have all resources ready. This is obvious. If you fail here, pupils quickly become frustrated and off-task.

Write up the lesson objective on the board. This acts as a constant reminder of what you are expecting pupils to have achieved by the end of the lesson.

Arrive at the lesson on time. No, don't linger for that second cup of coffee in the staff room. The chaos that may greet you won't be worth it, and it is poor modelling.

"Oh go on then. Just one more cup of coffee..."

Establish a procedure for entering the classroom. This will vary according to your situation. It may be wise to line pupils up outside first, or it may be appropriate for them to enter the classroom where you are waiting to receive them. Whatever your preference, it is the established routine that is important.

Seat pupils appropriately. Devise a seating plan based on separating potential troublemakers. The behaviour of troublesome individuals may be entirely dependent on the surrounding pupils.

Make certain you mark pupils' work regularly and on time. The quickest way to demotivate pupils is to give out books when you have not marked previous work. They will not see the point of getting on with new work.

You

Ensure that you take care of yourself. Make sure that your own lifestyle is one that will help you to be fit, healthy and as stress-free as possible. This is a really important point. Teaching is a very demanding, and as well as having the knowledge and skills to deliver the lesson, you need to be physically and emotionally up to the job. If you are very stressed, you will not be able to handle stressful situations in the class. It is your responsibility to de-stress yourself. Do whatever it takes. Join a gym? See a therapist? Go to yoga? Become a Buddhist? Eat raw vegetables?

And ... smile! Remember, every day is a new day, and you must learn to enter the classroom with a smile on your face and your head held high. Any worries and concerns must be left outside the classroom door. There will be plenty of time to deal with those later – and it is important that you have your own source of personal support to help deal with any anxieties you may have. If not, they can overwhelm you and get in the way of the very demanding job you have chosen to undertake.

Finally, as part of our preparation, we need to examine the role of the TA.

The role of the teaching assistant: managing for good behaviour

Ways in which TAs may assist with the management of behaviour

Sitting near pupils who find it difficult to stay on task	
Removing pupils from class at the teacher's request to offer them an opportunity to calm down	
Walking around the classroom to act as an extra pair of eyes	
Completing behaviour checklists to identify particular behaviour patterns of pupils	
Acting as a behaviour monitor by writing down names of pupils who misbehave	
Observing potential trouble and stepping in to act as mediator	
Making non-verbal signs to pupils, such as a stern look, frown or hand movement (verbal comments may interrupt lessons)	
Talking to pupils about their behaviour to explain why it is unacceptable	
Clarifying work when the pupil is confused	
Encouraging pupils to stay on task through the use of praise	
Having a quiet word in the ear of a pupil who is off-task	

Encouraging pupils to stay on task by offering positive comments in appropriate situations, such as when they have: • come into the class quietly • brought back homework • completed a piece of work neatly/quickly accurately • been kind to another child – or adult • listened well • followed instructions • been polite to a visitor to the school • remembered books or swimming/sports gear • contributed to the lesson • read well • brought something in from home for the lesson • succeeded with an activity out of school • worn their school uniform • arrived on time (if this is a problem).	
Additional ways in which support can be offered	

The role of the teaching assistant

The growing numbers of TAs employed in schools and their increasingly important role should mean that teachers are provided with an ally and a source of valuable support in the management of behaviour in the classroom. One of the problems encountered by TAs is that they are often unsure of their role in relation to behaviour management. Can they discipline pupils? Apply sanctions? Offer rewards? Teachers themselves are sometimes confused about how to manage their assistants. The list on page 37 describes ways in which TAs may be deployed. This list may be used as a form of contract between teachers and TAs. Together, check the points that apply. The resulting list then forms a contract, understood by and acceptable to both parties – which makes for clarity for all concerned. Further points may be added as befits your particular situation.

Essential strategies for good relationships

We hear a lot about strategies when behaviour management is on the agenda. To be honest, the word makes me cringe a bit. If only it were that simple! Strategies will not be worth the paper they are written on and will not work if teachers fail to build good relationships with their pupils. Let's face it, most pupils are very easy to like and relationships with them are easy. The biggest challenge is to hit it off with Amy, whose frequent off-the-wall behaviour challenges any teacher. In this situation, it is important to distinguish between Amy and her behaviour. It is Amy's behaviour you dislike, not Amy. But one thing is certain: if Amy has no respect or liking for her teacher, she will not respond to 'strategies'.

What are these magical strategies? Most of the time they are simply your own common-sense approach. Ask an effective teacher what strategies they employ, and they would find it difficult to name them. They are just part of how they teach, intuitively – but they certainly will be using strategies. Remember the four stages of learning outlined in Chapter 1? The unconsciously competent teachers 'don't know that they know'. They just do it. But please remember: effective teachers are not only using strategies.

Let's observe one of these teachers at work and see for ourselves what strategies and tactics she uses to maintain relationships with her more demanding pupils. Let me introduce Miss Awesome. She has been asked to take over a class who have become very disruptive. Their previous teacher has been absent frequently with health problems, and had not been able to deal with the class confidently. She has suddenly left the school. In the meantime, the class has become a challenge for anyone. Supply teachers have left after a morning. Crisis point has been reached. Enter, Miss Awesome.

Classroom action	Strategies at work
## Classroom entry Pupils enter the classroom under the watchful eye of Mrs Noble, the teaching assistant who has been allocated to support Miss Awesome with this class. They sit down with Miss Awesome watching (and smiling) from the front of the room. She has previously written up a short task on the board to act as a starter, and pupils know they are expected to tackle the task immediately. Mrs Noble walks around the room, ensuring pupils are on task. After two minutes Miss Awesome asks pupils for their attention, welcomes them, and asks briefly how they got on with the activity. Then the lesson begins. All is well. Miss Awesome knows some of the pupils in this class have become very challenging. It is her second session with them and she has made very careful preparations. She has been meticulous with her planning and differentiation, all the resources are ready, and the TA has been given copies of the plans and knows just what she has to do. Today, she is to sit with a group of more able pupils and support them with some extension activities. Miss Awesome has also devised a strategic seating plan which ensures, for example, that Tracy and Wayne are sitting as far apart from each other as possible. She has spare pencils and resources for pupils who may not have bought them to the class. She has also spent some time in the classroom taking down old and tatty wall displays, ready for new work. She has hung up the school rules in a prominent position. She has bought in a vase of flowers. The TA stands at the back of the room, watching for pupils who begin to talk or are off-task.	### Preventive measures ○ *TA support from the school* ○ *Lesson plans detailed and activities well differentiated* ○ *Stimulating starter activity ready* ○ *Well-established procedure for entry to classroom in place* ○ *All resources checked and ready for use* ○ *Previous meeting with TA, who is clear about her role* ○ *Seating plan* ○ *Spare resources* ○ *Pleasing environment* ○ *Support of TA with the management of general classroom behaviour*
## Starting the lesson – getting attention Now it is time for the lesson (maths) to begin. Some of the pupils are chattering while Miss Awesome attempts to outline the lesson objectives. She stops talking. She stays calm and waits for their attention. She is not smiling now. They are challenging her authority. After a minute, when pupils are showing no sign of settling down, she swings into action. She makes eye contact with the offenders, then says, 'Well done, Gemma and Natasha, for remembering to come in and get straight on with your work.' The offenders who are still talking receive the full benefit of her deadly stare.	○ *Having a clear outline of what is going to happen and the expected outcome* ○ *Making eye contact with offending pupils* ○ *Congratulating pupils who are on task*

Classroom action	Strategies at work
Some pupils carry on chatting. Manchester United were playing the previous night! She raises her hand. (She had previously told them when that happens they must do the same and give her their complete attention.) Only half the class respond.	● *Using a non-verbal reminder, previously established with the class*
Miss Awesome says, in a firm but not angry voice, 'I want you all to stop talking and look this way.'	● *Using a verbal reminder of what is expected*
Some hard-core offenders persist with the chatter. Miss Awesome has exhausted her repertoire of non-confrontational strategies, and moves on to the next phase: the sanctions.	
She raises her voice slightly, but does not shout. 'There are some pupils in this class who, sadly for the rest of you who are waiting quietly, have decided for their own particular reasons to break the class rules. I am going to keep everyone in at break time – one minute for every minute you keep me waiting. Mrs Noble is also watching to see who is deciding to break the rules. Those pupils must remember their chatter will lead to punishment for everyone, and perhaps they need to think about that.'	**Lower-order sanctions** ● *Peer-group support* ● *TA support*
Miss Awesome says this calmly, and indicates on the board every time a minute passes. In this way she is enlisting the support of pupils who will put pressure on the troublemakers to get back on task, as they too will suffer the consequences of the misbehaviour.	
This whole-class approach also means Miss Awesome avoids confrontation with the offenders. Chris was hoping to have an opportunity for his regular whinge of 'It ain't fair. You're always pickin' on me!' No chance!	● *Carrying out the identified sanction*
Finally, after three minutes, she is able to begin the lesson.	
Persistent shouting out Chris and Jamie keep shouting out the answers to the questions, instead of waiting with raised hands. Miss Awesome ignores them, asks only pupils with hands up, and thanks them for remembering the school rule.	● *Ignoring negative behaviour, congratulating the positive*
She engages offending pupils with eye contact and simply points to the school rule displayed on the wall that says 'Pupils to raise hands when answering or asking question or wishing to make a comment or contribution to the lesson'.	● *Using eye contact and non-verbal reminder of the rule*
Chris and Jamie persist in shouting out. Miss Awesome speaks directly to them: 'Chris and Jamie, I notice you seem to have forgotten the school rule about shouting out in class. I need to make sure you have remembered it. Tell me what you think it is, and if you don't know, I will ask other members of the class to remind you of it.'	● *Asking offenders for verbal clarification of the rule*
They each repeat the rule to Miss Awesome, who says 'Well done. Now follow it, please.'	

Classroom action	Strategies at work

The offender ignores all warnings

When Chris continues to shout out the answers, she says, 'Chris, I know you are aware of the rule, and you are choosing to break it. Now I am going to give you a choice. If you decide to shout out again, you will be choosing to work on your own at the back of the class. If your choice is to stay here with the others, then you follow the rule. What is your choice? You want to stay here? That's a good choice, and you know what you have to do.'

○ *Using language of choice: offenders must take responsibility for their chosen sanction if they break the rule – they have been given a choice*

It appears that Chris does not know, so he is asked to move. 'Chris, you have broken the rule, which means you are choosing to sit at the back. Take your things and move over there. Thank you.'

○ *Enforcing the sanction when the rule has been broken*

But Chris refuses to move! Miss Awesome groans inwardly. (She is human, after all.) She is really having a bad day and is having to pull out all the stops. But she knows this is important. She is establishing her high expectations and starting to win the respect of the rest of the class, who will see she means what she says.

Miss Awesome keeps repeating, 'Chris, you have chosen to sit at the back.'

'Yes, but ... no, but ... yes, but ... no, but ... '
'Chris, you have chosen to sit at the back.'
'Yes, but ... no, but ... yes, but ... no, but ... '
'Chris, you have chosen to sit at the back.'
'Yes, but ... no, but ... yes, but ... no, but ... '
'Chris, you have chosen to sit at the back.'

○ *The broken record technique, which means issuing the same instruction repeatedly, and not listening to the response*

Chris won't move to the back. He really is having a difficult day, so Miss Awesome moves on to the next phase: she brings in the troops.

Higher-order sanctions

Miss Awesome knows if she sends anyone outside without supervision, they are likely to run off or make faces through the classroom door. She has set up an arrangement with Mrs Co-operative in the adjoining classroom, so that in the event of needing to remove pupils from the class, she can send them there, with work, under the eye of that teacher. This sanction is only to be used on rare occasions, and the arrangement is reciprocal. Miss Awesome asks Mrs Noble to accompany Chris to the class next door. He folds his arms, looks at the floor and refuses to move. Oh no!

○ *Supervised removal from the class*

○ *Support from another teacher*

○ *Support from TA*

Miss Awesome sends a pupil to bring the designated member of the SMT to remove the offender. Her school behaviour policy ensures she knows just whom to contact in this situation. Chris is removed and the class is at peace. Miss Awesome thanks the rest of the class for waiting patiently and gets on with the lesson.

○ *Enlisting direct support from SMT member, an option to be used only when all else has failed*

The bell goes. Miss Awesome and Mrs Noble wait while the class file out, then go off to the staff room for a well-earned cup of tea. Miss Awesome knows that when the class have become used to accepting the rules, their behaviour and learning will improve and her job will become much, much easier.

Classroom action	Strategies at work
Verbal abuse of another pupil Miss Awesome returns, refreshed and invigorated by her cup of weak tea, two biscuits (digestives) and stimulating staff room chat, which is a good thing as her troubles are not yet over. Mrs Noble has to go off to another class to attend to an emergency there. She walks into the class to hear Jamie (Yes, him again!) cruelly taunting Pete, who wears glasses. 'Jamie, I am very surprised to hear you talking to Pete like that. You know the rule in this class is we treat each other with respect. I don't want to hear you speaking like that to Pete, or anyone else in this class, again. Is that clear?'	● *Ensuring own personal needs are met* ● *Expressing concern about the individual's behaviour – in this way, the behaviour, not the pupil, is criticised*
Failure to give in homework Miss Awesome now asks for the homework pupils were meant to complete. Sandip hasn't bought it to school. She investigates: 'Sandip, the school rule is you bring your homework back the next day. This is the third time you have failed to stick to that rule, so I need to discuss this matter further with you. See me later. Thank you.' Later, she will find out from Sandip if there are any problems with doing the homework – such as difficulties at home, or no suitable place for quiet study. If there is no problem, then a warning, which precedes a sanction (stay in at break), will be applied.	● *Delivering verbal reminder of the school rule* ● *Investigating a problem* ● *Threat of a sanction if no satisfactory explanation*
Wanderers The lesson commences, but some pupils leave their seats and wander around. She selects the main offender. 'Liam, is there a problem with your chair? Too hard? Too soft? I notice you have an extreme reluctance to stay in it. What's the problem? There isn't one? OK, sit down, and next time you need to leave your seat, put your hand up and ask me. Thank you.'	● *Using humour*

Classroom action	Strategies at work
A forgotten PE kit The class are due to go to PE. Kylie does not have her kit. 'Kylie, you know the rule about making sure you have your PE kit on Thursdays. This is the third time you have forgotten it. You can borrow kit today, but I want to talk to you about it after the lesson.' Later, Miss Awesome conducts another private investigation and, if there is not a satisfactory explanation, she will warn Kylie she will have to stay in at break. It is lunchtime now. The class line up quietly and the lunchtime supervisor comes to collect them. Miss Awesome returns to the staff room, where she eats her healthy lunch, relaxes with the staff and recharges her batteries. She is looking forward to going to the gym that night to let off steam.	○ *Having spare resources ready* ○ *Creating opportunity for private discussion in case there is a good reason for breaking the rule* ○ *Support from well-trained lunchtime supervisor* ○ *Interesting playground* ○ *Extra-curricular activities available* ○ *Healthy lunch provided*
Restlessness and short-attention spans The next lesson is one in which Miss Awesome needs the class to sit still and listen. She knows some pupils find it very difficult to sit still for any period of time. They find it easier to concentrate for short periods, followed by a brief break with an opportunity to leave their seats if possible. Her lesson plans reflect this. But two of the pupils are very restless, so Miss Awesome provides them with permissible objects to manipulate – a worry ball or roll of Blu-Tack®. This allows pupils to concentrate on what she is saying, with their fidgeting focused on an object rather than disturbing fellow pupils.	○ *Giving pupils permission to fidget with a specified object, which helps them to concentrate and carry on listening without disturbing others*
A pupil leaves the class without permission In the meantime, Miss Awesome notices that Kylie is crying. When she asks what is wrong, Kylie suddenly stands up and runs out of the class. There is no TA available to follow, so Miss Awesome has to send a pupil for an SMT member. She knows immediate action is needed. She would have sent the TA (if there were one) to persuade the pupil to remain on the premises and inform the SMT immediately.	○ *There is no hierarchy of sanctions to run through here. Immediate action is needed*
A noisy latecomer Delia, who left the class a few minutes previously, legitimately, you will be pleased to hear, now returns to the room, and deliberately interrupts the lesson by shouting about something she has just seen. Miss Awesome needs to deal with it. 'I thought World War Three had started, Delia. Go back outside and come in quietly. Thank you.'	○ *Uses humour to deflate the situation*

Classroom action	Strategies at work
Deliberate annoyance The class now get on with the writing task. Some of the pupils start to make silly noises. Miss Awesome tries ignoring them, but it continues, so she has to tackle it head-on. 'Some pupils are choosing to make a noise which is preventing me and the rest of the class from getting on with our work. If it happens again, I will keep the class behind to complete the work.' Some of the class glare at the offenders, who then quieten down and get on with the task.	● *Tactical ignoring* ● *Use of peer-group pressure*
Physical abuse of a teacher or TA Just as Miss Awesome thinks she is beginning to get to grips with the class, she hears shouting from outside the door. Now what? Gritting her teeth, she looks into the corridor, and sees two boys fighting. She raises her voice: 'Stop it!' But one of the boys pushes her roughly against the wall and runs off. Immediate action must be taken. Miss Awesome sends a pupil for a member of the SMT to come straight away, and brings the other boy into her class, asking him to calm down and wait quietly. He is a witness to the incident as well as a participant. Miss Awesome takes a deep breath and gets on stoically with the lesson. She knows the SMT will support her, and she will need to describe what happened later, as serious incidents need to be documented. At last, the bell goes for afternoon break and the pupils make an orderly exit from the classroom. This cheers Miss Awesome. At least they are getting the message about procedures for entry and exit to the classroom. And at least everyone survived. She knew it was going to be difficult to bring the class round and she knew it would not be possible to achieve this without the help she is receiving.	● *Sanction is now responsibility of SMT, who immediately send for parents. Since this is a first offence for this boy, he is likely to be suspended from school for two days. Long-term offenders may face permanent exclusion* ● *Well-established procedures for classroom exit*
Arguing with the teacher After break, all the class enter the room quietly, sit down and get on with the task. 'Light at the end of the tunnel,' thinks Miss Awesome. She asks Robert to take the register to the secretary. It is his turn that day to perform any tasks the teacher may need, giving out books and so on. Kylie intervenes, saying she wants to take it and it's her turn today. But the list on the wall clearly indicates it is Robert's turn, and Miss Awesome points this out to Kylie. She will not listen. Miss Awesome does not allow arguing, and she stands her ground: Kylie: You said I could take the register. Miss Awesome: No, I didn't. It's your turn tomorrow, Kylie. Kylie: You did!	● *Clear lists of class responsibilities, on prominent display, to avoid confusion* ● *Broken record technique*

Classroom action	Strategies at work
Miss Awesome: It's your turn tomorrow, Kylie. Kylie: You said I could take the register. Miss Awesome: It's your turn tomorrow, Kylie. Kylie: It ain't fair! Miss Awesome: It's your turn tomorrow, Kylie. Kylie gives in.	
Damage to property The class seem much more settled; they are beginning to understand that Miss Awesome means business. They are starting to feel respect for her and observe she is firm but kind. She remains approachable and they are starting to like her. However, before she can finally escape to her home for rest and recuperation, there is a further incident. George tries to take the history book from Claire. He grabs at it and the cover is ripped off. Miss Awesome steps in: 'George, you have just torn your textbook. School will need to replace that and so a letter will go home to your parents, unless you manage to repair it so it is fit to be used by other pupils. At the end of the lesson, take it with you, and if it is returned to me tomorrow in a reasonable state, no further action will be taken.' The rest of the afternoon passes quietly, and at last the pupils leave the class in an orderly manner, Miss Awesome smiling at them as they leave and wishing them well. She wants them to leave with a good feeling. As soon as peace reigns, she sits down, and congratulates herself on an exhausting, but successful day. The head comes down to see how things have gone, asks if she needs any additional support, and thanks her for all her efforts. Miss Awesome feels appreciated by her school and this increases her motivation to carry on with the difficult task of transforming a disruptive class into an orderly one. Well done, Miss Awesome.	○ *Asking pupil to take responsibility for any damage they have caused* ○ *Applying a sanction if the damage is deliberate and irreparable – for example, a letter sent home, requesting some contribution to replace the article* ○ *Support and encouragement from SMT*

This model of response contains ideas that may be used in different situations, but it has to be based on the existence of a strong support system in school. All teachers must know what to do when the behaviour of one or more pupils gets beyond their control. The very knowledge that such a system exists provides all teachers with confidence, knowing that, whatever happens, there is a structure in place upon which they can rely. This confidence will be reflected in the teacher's body language. An assertive teacher is far less likely to incur problem behaviour than a teacher who is confused about what their options are. Forewarned is forearmed.

You may not agree with some of the strategies employed by Miss Awesome. Keeping all pupils in when only a few have misbehaved may be one of them. This is a tactic that can be used only very occasionally – and sometimes short, sharp, shock tactics need to be applied. You will have your own ideas, and what works for you will not necessarily work for others. You will need to experiment until you find strategies which are effective and which you feel comfortable with. It will be up to you.

Food for thought

A colleague was experiencing problems with the behaviour of a particular class, so the school sent her on a weekend behaviour management course. The course was inspirational. She learned many new strategies and arrived full of hope and confidence to take up the challenge on Monday morning. Her new positive approach, her smiles, her new dress, her newly introduced strategies, her subtle use of humour, seemed to work like a charm. The usually unruly class seemed quiet and settled. (Or watchful and suspicious.) Suddenly, a hand went up. 'Yes, Pavinder,' she said, yet another smile crossing her face, as recommended in the course. Pavinder responded. 'Scuse me, Miss. Don't mean to be rude or nothing, but 'ave you bin drinkin'?' The class exploded. Chaos reigned. Normality returned. The moral of the story? Introduce change gradually.

A few pearls of wisdom

Here are some further ideas for managing the relationship with pupils.

Avoid at all costs:

- ⊙ sarcasm;
- ⊙ humiliation;
- ⊙ displays of anger;
- ⊙ showing distress;
- ⊙ ignoring serious misdemeanours;
- ⊙ ignoring bullying;
- ⊙ introducing sanctions too early.

Sarcasm I now see to be, in general, the language of the devil; for which reason I have long since renounced it.

Thomas Carlyle

Mind your language

Language is a powerful tool. What you say and how you say it will elicit either a positive or a negative response. In Charlotte Bronte's *Jane Eyre*, Mr Brocklehurst, benefactor of Lowood School, where Jane was sent to complete her education, provides us with a good example of how not to deal with dysfunctional pupils. It appears that he believed the threat of purgatory might bring about improvement in behaviour. Here is Mr Brocklehurst's first encounter with Jane:

'No sight so sad as that of a naughty child,' he began, 'especially a naughty little girl. Do you know where the wicked go after death?'
'They go to hell,' was my ready and orthodox answer.
'And what is hell? Can you tell me that?'
'A pit full of fire.'
'And should you like to fall into that pit, and to be burning there for ever?'
'No sir.'
'What must you do to avoid it?'
I deliberated a moment; my answer, when it did come, was objectionable:
'I must keep in good health, and not die.'

Not the answer Mr Brocklehurst was seeking. The language you use in the classroom should include 'I' and not 'you' messages. Mr Brocklehurst was saying in essence, 'You are a naughty girl, Jane Eyre.' 'You' messages criticise the person rather than their behaviour. Such threatening language will result in 'fight or flight' behaviour. Jane fought! Here, with apologies to Charlotte Bronte, is the speech rephrased, with Mr Brocklehurst making use of 'I' messages. He values Jane as a human being, but is disappointed by her behaviour.

'I am concerned about your behaviour, Jane, and surprised too. Would you like to tell me what happened?'
I explained my side of the story.
'Thank you for your explanation, but it is clear you broke some of the school rules. I am very disappointed and surprised at what happened. I believed you to be a kind and considerate girl. I didn't expect this kind of behaviour from you.'
'I'm sorry, Mr Brocklehurst. It won't happen again.'
'Thank you for the apology, Jane. I appreciate that, but nevertheless you know there is a price to pay for rule breaking. You will need to stay behind for detention tomorrow.'

Note the different outcome. Here are further, current examples of positive talk.

Negative and critical	Positive and calming
Will you stop wandering around the class, Hayley! I am sick of it!	Hayley, get on with your work. Thank you. You only have five minutes left to complete the task.
Stop this awful noise, Year 7! You can be heard at the end of the corridor!	Thank you to all of those sitting quietly. I will wait for everyone else to follow your example.
You must not run down the corridor, you silly girl!	Please walk down the corridor. It can be dangerous if you run.
Late again, Amy! If this happens again, you will find yourself in detention. You waste my time, I will waste yours!	I am concerned about your lack of punctuality, Amy. I want you to arrive at school on time tomorrow and in the future, please. If there is a problem about that, please come and talk to me about it after the lesson.
Just look at the mess this group have left on their table!	I'd like the children in this group to return to their table and put everything away. Thank you.

Please say 'thank you'

You will note, in the final example above, that instead of using the polite word 'please' at the beginning of the request, the polite words 'thank you' have been added at the end. There is a reason for this. The words 'Please will you ...?' indicate a plea, a choice – to which the answer could be 'No'. It is more powerful to use the words 'thank you' at the end. This language assumes that the pupils will follow instructions for which you are politely thanking them. In this situation, you are not offering a choice.

Let the music play

Research has shown that playing music quietly, particularly Mozart, helps to keep children on task much longer, and also has a calming effect. For more on this, see books by Donald Campbell, including *The Mozart Effect for Children* (2002).

Mind your body language

The language of the body is powerful. Every time you communicate with pupils, you are saying a lot about yourself. Whatever is being said verbally will be supplemented by body language. To be powerful, you need to demonstrate positive body language, which is reflected in your:

- eye contact;
- facial expression;
- head movements;
- gestures and body movement;
- posture and stance;
- proximity and orientation;
- bodily contact;
- appearance and technique;
- timing and synchronisation.

In summary, keep it positive and look as if you know what you are doing. A confident walk, good eye contact, and appropriate facial expression all give out the silent message 'I am in charge here.' For more information, see Gordon Wainwright's *Teach Yourself Body Language* (2003).

Find your voice

Ensure your voice is clear and its tone interesting. Voices which are sharp, monotonous, too loud, or too low pitched can be a real turn-off. If you feel this is a problem, seek help. It is possible to train the voice to a more acceptable tone. It can be really useful to video a lesson to check out your body language and voice. You may not realise there is a problem until you see yourself in action.

Take an interest in pupils as individuals

'Right, Paul. Before we begin, just tell me one thing. How did your team get on in the big match on Saturday?' Taking an interest in individual pupils helps to establish a more personal relationship and encourages them to like you. 'Wow, Miss is taking an interest in me. She must like me!'

Share a little bit of your own life, too, but tell them about your dog and not your divorce.

> 'My big news, Year 7! I have just managed to get a ticket for the Wimbledon final. Wasn't that lucky? I'll tell you all about it next week. Now, let's get on with maths.'

"Well done, Gemma and Natasha!"

Positive intervention

Try to find as many ways as possible to interact positively with your class in order to create a happy and stimulating environment. I call this 'giving positive strokes'. A stroke is a unit of recognition. A stroke may be conditional, awarded on condition that some task or action is performed – in other words for 'doing' something – or they may be unconditional, when the pupil has to do nothing in return for the acknowledgement; they are rewarded for their 'being'.

Conditional (doing) strokes can be awarded for:

- ❍ bringing homework back on time;
- ❍ being kind to another child;
- ❍ picking up rubbish without being asked;
- ❍ helping another child;
- ❍ showing good manners;
- ❍ sitting up straight;
- ❍ good writing;
- ❍ trying hard with a particular subject;
- ❍ answering a question;
- ❍ wearing uniform;
- ❍ taking care of school resources;
- ❍ carrying out a task well.

The list is endless and will vary with the age and ability of the pupils. These 'doing' strokes are valuable, and their use helps to establish a positive classroom environment. For more on this, see *Improving Behaviour and Raising Self Esteem in the Classroom* (Barrow *et al.*, 2001).

Reward systems, which exist in all schools, build on the positive strokes approach. Pupils are encouraged to behave and to work well; in return, they receive a reward. It is important that reward systems are consistent, and that all teachers are aware of and make use of them. The rewards may include:

- ❍ awarding house points, stickers, certificates of achievement;
- ❍ sending letters, certificates or phone calls home;
- ❍ showing work in a good work assembly;
- ❍ having name inserted in the golden book;
- ❍ pupil of the week posters;
- ❍ verbal praise;
- ❍ written praise in books;
- ❍ having a privilege;
- ❍ being given a responsibility;
- ❍ being chosen to do something;
- ❍ marbles in jars for groups.

Food for thought

Rewards do not work for all pupils, particularly those who belong to the troubled group. There may be several reasons.

- ◒ Pupils who have learned to gain attention in negative ways, by rule breaking, not conforming and so on, do not want positive conditional strokes. It is bad for their image. They have established a bad boy or bad girl identity.
- ◒ Pupils with low self-esteem cannot accept them, as they do not believe they deserve them.
- ◒ Some pupils do not see the value of rewards and may regard them as manipulative.
- ◒ The type of reward may be important: some pupils may be interested in a reward that means a trip to a burger bar, but would throw a certificate of achievement into the nearest bin.

Again, the type of reward will depend on the age of the pupils. A Year 8 pupil is not going to be thrilled to receive and wear a sticker with the words, 'I am a good reader' or 'Star of the week'.

So, what will work for them? Answer: unconditional strokes.

Strokes for 'being' are even more valuable than strokes for 'doing', because they are unconditional. In other words, the pupils have to do nothing to achieve them, other than exist. They are an acknowledgment of a person's intrinsic value. For example, 'I like your new dress' and 'What lovely writing' are conditional. The person is valued for the dress or their writing, not for themselves. Unconditional strokes simply communicate 'I like you.' No conditions needed. These are strokes some of our more troubled pupils may never have received. They are our most valuable tools in our effort to build relationships with pupils.

Unconditional (being) strokes can be delivered by:

- ◒ smiling when pupils come into the class;
- ◒ a thumbs-up or wink at a pupil you see away from class;
- ◒ asking pupils how they are when they have been away from school;
- ◒ enquiring how their favourite football team got on last week;
- ◒ showing concern for personal problems (e.g. asking 'How is your granddad?' if he has been in hospital);
- ◒ saying at the end of a lesson, 'Hey, Year 8, I really enjoy teaching this class. Thanks for being such a great group';
- ◒ acknowledging pupils when you see them in the street;
- ◒ sharing a joke;
- ◒ using humour in class;
- ◒ sharing a bit of your own life with the pupils;
- ◒ remembering to say 'Happy birthday'.

On the whole, schools are very accomplished at dealing out 'doing' strokes, on which reward systems are based, but the value of the 'being' strokes often does not receive much acknowledgement. This is a pity because they are valuable, especially to troubled pupils. Consider your own practice and think carefully about how often you deliver these strokes. Maybe you will find your supply is inadequate. Maybe you can think up ways to increase it.

"Hey, Year 8, Thanks for being such a great group!"

And last but not least, humour

The use of humour is an important aspect. I took part in some research to assess the impact of permanent exclusion from school on pupils and their parents. The research, funded by the Nuffield Foundation, and resulting in Charlie Cooper's *Understanding School Exclusion* (2002), included interviewing a group of eight pupils who had been permanently excluded from their schools. All were asked to identify teachers with whom they had worked well. When interviewed, these particular teachers all mentioned the use of humour as crucial. Humour connects with pupils at a feelings level and helps them relate well to their teachers. Much of education, of course, is linked to pupils' thinking, but it is through feelings that we make connections. These teachers had been able to connect with highly dysfunctional pupils using humour, motivating them to stay on task and behave well. The pupils, who were disruptive in most lessons, behaved well with teachers who made the effort to develop a positive relationship with them. They said that these teachers:

- joke with them;
- have personality;
- care, listen and help;
- talk to you, say hello and help you if you are having problems;
- get involved and sit down with you;
- listen, understand and make learning fun.

These comments provide further evidence that the quality of the relationship is vital, and that who you are as a person is even more important than what you do as a teacher.

The mediocre teacher tells. The good teacher explains. The superior teacher demonstrates. The great teacher inspires.

William Arthur Ward

Chapter 5
Dealing with confrontation

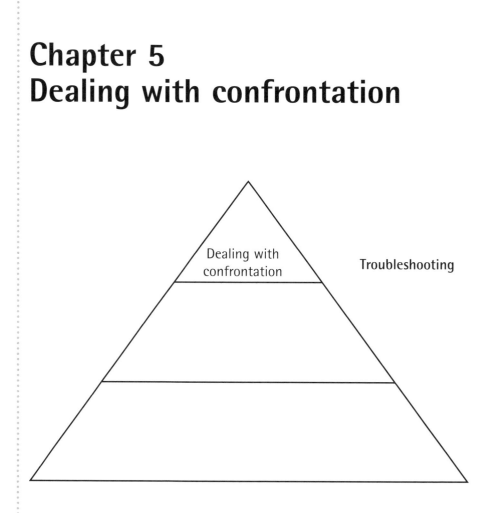

You are using the strategies, most of the class is responding well, and your confidence is growing. This, of course, will be reflected in your positive body language – and your class will respond accordingly. You no longer have to put on an act. However, conflict is bound to arise, so this chapter considers the best ways of dealing with it.

We know that, despite all the effort schools and teachers are putting in, situations of confrontation leading to conflict will occasionally occur. Pupils who are deliberately disobedient and threatening not only disrupt learning in the class, but also jeopardise the health and safety of other pupils. It is important that teachers do not exacerbate the situation. Conflict can occur as a result of mismanagement by the teacher or because the pupil concerned is uncontrollable and very upset.

Number 1 rule: avoid confrontation

Challenging pupils thrive on confrontation. It gives them an opportunity to take you on, receive your undivided attention for a while and dump some of their anger, inappropriately, onto you. It's also a good way to get the undivided attention of the whole class.

To illustrate how easy it is to fall into the trap laid by certain pupils, let us take a quick look at Miss Cross's classroom.

"You are late! Give me your CD player! You will stay behind for detention!"

Scenario 1: Miss Cross's class

Cassie Pugh is a Year 7 pupil with considerable emotional problems, who is easily upset and can be very aggressive and volatile. Today, she walks into class five minutes after the lesson has started, still wearing her coat, listening to her personal CD player. Judging by the expression on her face, she is clearly upset and angry – in fact, probably looking for trouble.

Miss Cross: Cassie Pugh, you are late! (*confrontation*) Take off your coat (*confrontation*) and go outside and hang it up. (*confrontation*) Give me your CD player (*confrontation*) and note that you will stay behind for detention after school. (*confrontation*)

Cassie: *Ignores the teacher and sits down wearing her coat. She slowly takes some gum from its wrapper, and places it slowly and tantalisingly into her mouth.* (*confrontation*)

Miss Cross: (*inwardly groaning*) How dare you ignore me! (*confrontation*) Do as you are told immediately! (*confrontation*)

Cassie: *Throws the gum wrapper at her mate Jodie,* (*confrontation*) *who responds by throwing a pencil back at Cassie.* (*confrontation*) *The disruption rapidly spreads.*

The class: *A mixed response. The group who are anxious to succeed become frustrated and angry that Miss Cross cannot control the class, and feel hostile towards her. What a waste of precious time! The other group, always looking for any excuse to avoid work, are enjoying this opportunity to have a break, and join in or observe the ensuing battle happily. Neither group feels respect for Miss Cross.*

This lesson will end in one of three ways:

① Miss Cross has to send a pupil to fetch a member of the SMT to calm the class down and remove the major players.
Not a good situation. Miss Cross has lost respect and it is seen that she can't manage without support. She feels ashamed.

② Miss Cross struggles on with increasing disruption, not wanting the humiliation of involving anyone else. She does not want other staff members to know she is unable to cope.
She knows and the class know she isn't coping. The lesson objective has not been achieved. She feels anxious and dreads the next lesson.

③ She breaks down in tears and leaves the class, heading for the doctor's and six weeks' absence leave owing to stress. This lesson was the final straw.
She feels a complete failure. She may blame the school and the system and not take responsibility for her own inadequacies, or she may reflect, take responsibility, admit she needs more support and seek help from the school. She could read some behaviour management books, and ask if she can have additional training, and she could observe competent teachers in their classrooms. She needs to have a fresh start and an action plan.

He who establishes his argument by noise and command shows that his reason is weak.

Michael de Montaigne

Now, we'll look at another classroom and observe the same situation, but with a different approach. Let's see what happens with Mrs Gentle.

Scenario 2: Mrs Gentle's class

Cassie Pugh walks into class five minutes after the lesson has started, still wearing her coat, listening to her personal CD player, and clearly upset and angry. Mrs Gentle is immediately aware of the situation and feels sorry for Cassie. She knows Cassie has a tough time at home, but is also a bit afraid of her temper. Mrs Gentle hates scenes. She ignores the situation and carries on talking to the class. (The passive approach: if I don't do anything, it may go away.) The class notice Cassie is breaking the rules and feel she is being favoured.

"Er ...would you like to put the CD away, dear?"

| Jodie: | Please miss! Cassie is listening to her CD player. Can I bring mine to school? |
| Mrs Gentle: | No, of course not, Jodie. Put your CD player away, Cassie dear. It may get damaged. (*She opts for the nice, sympathetic approach.*) |

| Cassie: | *Takes no notice of her. Mrs Gentle carries on ignoring her, carries on being passive. Cassie slowly takes some gum from its wrapper and places it tantalisingly into her mouth. Mrs Gentle ignores her.* |

The class grow unsettled. She is breaking another rule and getting away with it! It's not fair! They begin to lose respect for the teacher, interest in the lesson diminishes and the noise level increases. Someone tries to snatch the CD player, which ends up on the floor, damaged. Cassie's smug expression now changes and rage takes over. She throws the CD player against the wall. Some pupils in the class laugh as it breaks. Mrs Gentle, at last, realises she has to intervene.

| Mrs Gentle: | How unkind to laugh! Cassie, pick it up and give it to me. I will see if it can be mended. |

Cassie storms out of the room, leaving Mrs Gentle wondering what she did wrong. She had been so kind and understanding. The class has descended into chaos.

Passivity is not the answer either. Knowing which behaviour to ignore and when to intervene is an important part of managing behaviour. Tactical ignoring is a very different matter from ignoring everything. And yet, I have observed teachers who teach in this way, completely oblivious to the impact on the class. Unconscious incompetence, do you think? (See Chapter 2.)

Finally, let's see what happens when an assertive approach is adopted.

Scenario 3: Mr Smart's class

Cassie Pugh walks into class five minutes after the lesson has started, still wearing her coat, listening to her personal CD player, and clearly upset and angry. Mr Smart is immediately aware that this is potentially a confrontational situation and takes steps to avoid it.

At first he ignores her (opening non-confrontational move) while he finishes off what he is saying to the class. Then, without looking at Cassie Pugh, he speaks to the whole class.

"Oh, just a reminder, Year 7. The rule is no CD players in school ..."

Mr Smart: Just a reminder, Year 7, that the school rule is no CD players to be brought onto the school premises and coats to be taken off before entering the class. (*second non-confrontational move*) If you are wearing your coat or have your CD player with you, I will generously give you three minutes to remove the coat and put the CD player on my desk. (*third non-confrontational move*) I should also remind you that in this class, breaking rules today means a detention tomorrow. (*fourth non-confrontational move, which also introduces a bit of humour*)

Mr Smart carries on with the lesson. He has not fallen into the confrontation trap and, with a bit of luck, Cassie – who has clearly failed in gaining the negative attention she was hoping for – will sidle off to hang up her coat and quietly place her CD player on the desk. She does not have to lose face in front of the class as she was given some time to think things through, and at no time was she personally identified. Mr Smart has dealt with the lawbreaker and has maintained the respect of his class.

Loose end: Cassie was late

A quiet word in the ear later in the lesson should address the lateness issue, but in a compassionate manner: 'Is there a problem that caused you to be late, Cassie?' If there isn't a good reason, then the agreed school sanction must be imposed. This way, confrontation has been avoided and Cassie has got the message that her tactics don't work. She is unlikely to employ them in that class in the future. It's a bit like a bully seeking a victim. When bullies find victims they can scare or upset, they will torment them again and again. The same rule applies to teachers. You need to develop the sensitive approach, but it will only work if the sensitivity comes from a genuine concern for the pupil. However, an understanding of Cassie's complex home circumstances does not mean you accept low standards of behaviour, as in Mrs Gentle's approach. This is patronising and ultimately detrimental to the pupil, who will recognise they are being treated differently. It will emphasise for them that they are different, and therefore inadequate. A good relationship with Cassie is essential if you are to maintain control, but maintain the same high expectations for her as you do for the rest of the class.

It is important that you see through the hostile and disrespectful approach of pupils such as Cassie.

Even when a situation becomes so personal, even if others insult you directly, it has nothing to do with you. What they say, what they do and the opinions they give are according to the agreements they have in their own minds. Their point of view comes from all the programming they have received during domestication.

Don Miguel Ruiz,
The Four Agreements

"Don't worry, I'm not taking this personally."

See through the hidden agenda

Often, fear of allowing people to get close to them will mean that pupils with challenging behaviour use hostility and anti-social behaviour to keep you – and other people – at a distance. They are looking for a place to dump their accumulated internal anger, often inappropriately. That place may be you. Don't take things personally. It is easy to believe, when you have been verbally abused or mimicked by pupils, that they dislike you, and this can be upsetting and undermine your confidence. It is important to understand that some pupils want you to feel bad, because it gives them some power and allows them to off-load some of their anger on you. Don't take that on board by becoming their victim. It is not good for you or them as it reinforces their belief that the only way to be powerful is to hurt others. If you do not respond to them, you do not give them power. If taking things personally is an issue, you might find it helpful to read Don Miguel Ruiz's *The Four Agreements* (1997).

Find other ways of helping children release their anger. Physical activity can help. Unfortunately, opportunities for PE and games are now limited in our largely academic curriculum. Also, many pupils are now taken to school in the car rather than walking, further diminishing the opportunities for physical activity. It's worth remembering never to deny a games lesson as a form of punishment.

The alternatives for the management of anger include anger management classes, counselling or some other form of therapy, but often waiting lists are long and usually the pupil has to agree to attend.

What you can do, however, is let them have you on their side. Try to see through their tactics.

Angela Devlin, whose research is published in *Criminal Classes* (1997), looked at young people who experienced severe deprivation as children, many of whom ended up in prison. Her particular question was about those who did not go to prison: what was it that made the difference? Her research showed that it was often a significant adult, and often that adult was a teacher. Teachers should not underestimate the effect and personal influence they may have on their pupils. Stop and consider your own situation for a moment. Was there a teacher who played a significant part in your life?

An assertive approach

We have examined three possible approaches teachers may choose to take. Miss Cross opted for the aggressive stance, Mrs Gentle went for the passive approach, while Mr Smart smartly adopted the assertive stance.

Aggression may facilitate some kind of punitive control, but it is at the expense of the relationship, and the quality of work produced by pupils will be affected. It will be completed because they have to do it, not because they want to.

Passivity, when teachers do not take account of disruptive behaviour which needs to be addressed, usually leads to general, low-level, ongoing disruption with frequent escalations into high-level disruption. The quality of work produced is unsatisfactory and pupils' attitude to the subject is influenced. Assertive behaviour usually results in pupils respecting and liking the teacher, and producing work and behaviour from a sense of motivation and enjoyment and a desire to please.

The most successful teachers are the ones who adopt the assertive approach. To see the differences between the three approaches, read through the following examples and identify the position the teacher is taking. The answers will probably be fairly clear, but can be checked on page 60.

A pupil shouts out answers instead of putting their hand up

The teacher	The class
Ignores the situation.	The pupil carries on shouting out the answers, and the rest of the class learn that rule breaking is allowed. They join in the shouting out, or lose interest and give up.
Shouts at the pupil, and uses sarcasm and public humiliation as a means of persuading them to submit to the rules.	The pupil may conform, but inwardly feels anger and resentment towards the teacher. They will not attempt to answer any more questions. The class feel troubled by the teacher's hostile approach, thinking this could happen to them. The teacher loses respect.
Reminds the whole class that the rule is to put hands up before answering questions. If the problem persists, the individual is reminded. If it continues, a sanction is applied.	The class are reminded of the rule and observe the teacher taking action. They learn that they cannot break rules and get away with it. The pupil in trouble retains their dignity as the teacher has not shouted or humiliated them, When they do put their hand up, they are congratulated on remembering the rule this time.

A pupil is late – again

The teacher	The class
Makes a mental note that the pupil has arrived late again, and with a look indicates the pupil is to sit down quietly, but does not interrupt the lesson. When the class are settled, the teacher quietly reminds the pupil that a rule has been broken again and asks if extenuating circumstances were the cause. If not, the sanction will be applied.	Are not interrupted by the appearance of the latecomer, but note that the teacher takes action to deal with the broken rule. This will remind them that if they break rules, they will have to face the consequences. The teacher gains respect. The latecomer has been dealt with sensitively and will continue to respect the teacher, despite the sanction.
Ignores the fact that the pupil is late again.	The late appearance disturbs the class, who note that no action is taken and that there is no motivation for them to be on time either. The latecomer has no incentive to be on time in the future.
Reprimands the pupil the minute they enter, and tells them in front of the whole class that they will be placed in detention.	The lesson has been disturbed and the latecomer is likely to respond angrily to the way they have been criticised. They do not want to lose face in front of the class. A time-wasting battle between teacher and pupil is likely to follow. Lesson targets are not achieved.

A pupil keeps talking in class

The teacher	The class
Ignores the pupil.	The offender produces virtually no work. There is also a detrimental effect on the quality of work produced by the pupils around them and, to a lesser extent, on the rest of the class.
Shouts at the pupil every time they talk.	This interrupts the flow of the lesson and distracts the rest of the class at regular intervals. It has an impact on the quality of the work produced by the whole class. Noisy teachers create noisy classes.
Reminds the whole class of the school rule and asks them to say why the rule is important. If the talking continues, then individual intervention is necessary; the pupil is reminded of the rule and the sanction that will be applied if necessary.	The class does not suffer as a result of one child's behaviour. They are all reminded of the significance of the rule, but can also judge the teacher is not a soft option and will deal with rule breakers. This means they are less likely to break rules themselves.

It is clear that the assertive approach wins each time. In order to achieve this, you will need to be confident that discipline can be maintained without resorting to the raised voice. Keep the tone of your voice clear and calm, even when dealing with difficult pupils, as this is far more likely to keep the pupil engaged in some sort of dialogue with you. When you do feel it is necessary to raise your voice on certain rare occasions, it will be a powerful tool. Also, watch your body language. Maintain eye contact with your pupils and stand tall. Show them who is in charge.

We have explored a positive approach to dealing with behaviour, but of course pupils do need a clear framework which establishes just what is expected of them. They also need to know what to expect when they break the rules.

Hierarchy of measures and sanctions

All schools will have sanctions in place. There should be a hierarchy of measures and sanctions at both school (SMT) and classroom level. The classroom sanctions will be deployed only after a hierarchy of other measures has been tried, and has failed. School sanctions are brought into play only when classroom sanctions have proved ineffective.

Here is an example of a three-tier system of measures and sanctions.

A hierarchy of classroom measures

In response to a minor incident, such as a pupil talking when they should be listening, the teacher will:

- give the offending pupil a look;
- issue a reminder to the whole class about the relevant classroom rule;
- give the individual a tap on the shoulder, or use eye contact, or another look;
- have a word in the pupil's ear;
- give a reminder of the sanction (moving to another seat to sit alone);
- deliver the sanction.

Classroom sanctions

These could include:

- removing the pupil to another part of the class;
- writing the pupil's name on the board;
- loss of a privilege;
- missing a play/break time;
- cleaning up a mess they have made, in their own time;
- completing unfinished work in their own time;
- removing the pupil to another class for a short period (with prior agreement from the teacher);
- sending the pupil to another teacher, the headteacher, or a TA to show unsatisfactory work;

- detention;
- removal from the class to a specified area;
- withdrawal of lunchtime privileges;
- withholding participation in any school trips or sports events that are not essential to the curriculum;
- withdrawal from a particular lesson or group to work in isolation;
- completion of assigned or extra work in own time.

A hierarchy of school sanctions

When the application of a classroom sanction proves inadequate and the behaviour is more severe, external school sanctions need to be applied. These will include:

- sending the pupil to the behaviour co-ordinator or headteacher;
- carrying out a useful task in the school, such as removing graffiti;
- a letter home;
- detention;
- temporary exclusion;
- permanent exclusion.

Detention is allowed if:

- the school behaviour policy or rules list it as a possible sanction;
- it is reasonable in the circumstances;
- the school gives 24 hours' written notice to the parents;
- the parent has not withdrawn consent for their child to be given detention.

Sanctions are necessary because they establish firm boundaries, which help pupils feel secure. But don't forget that the healthy school always focuses on its rewards and has to resort to its sanctions very rarely.

In this chapter we have explored ways of dealing with confrontation. If you have found yourself in a classroom situation that is difficult to handle, or felt dissatisfaction at the outcome, then it may be helpful to reflect afterwards on your approach, asking yourself these simple questions:

- What happened?
- What did I do?
- Was there anything I could have done differently?

This is how we learn. It's about looking at the options and making sure that next time we are in a position to select the appropriate one. This is how Miss Awesome became Miss Awesome and Mr Smart became Mr Smart. Both were committed to what they were doing and took steps to ensure they became really effective.

Final thoughts

I hope you have found this book useful – whether it has provided reassurance that you are on the right track or whether you have learned some effective new strategies from it. Whatever use you have made of it, the message is simple: we can all only do the best we can. We live in difficult times, and maybe the patterns of increasingly disruptive behaviour we are encountering in schools are a refection of that. I used to think when I was young and innocent that I could change the world. Now I know that perhaps all I can do is have a positive effect on some young people, which may affect the course of their lives in a positive way – just as a few people, some of them teachers, had a positive impact on mine. That, in itself, is a big responsibility. It is a sobering thought that as teachers we are in a position where we can have a big impact on the life of another human being. It is a privileged position, and we must never forget it.

> Our deepest fear is not that we are inadequate, our deepest fear is that we are powerful beyond measure. It is our light, not our darkness that most frightens us.
>
> We ask ourselves, 'Who am I to be brilliant, gorgeous, talented and fabulous?' You are a child of God. Your playing small doesn't help the world. There is nothing enlightened by shrinking so that others won't feel insecure around us. We are born to manifest the glory of God that is within us. It is not just in some of us; it is in everyone. And as we let our own light shine, we are unconsciously giving permission for everyone to do the same. As we are liberated from our own fear, our presence automatically liberates others.
>
> Nelson Mandela

Surely teachers have been given more power than most to influence the world?

Answers for pages 57–8:

A pupil is continually shouting out answers instead of putting their hand up: passive, aggressive, assertive

A pupil is late – again: assertive, passive, aggressive

A pupil keeps talking in class: passive, aggressive, assertive

Resources

References

Barrow, G., Bradshaw, E. and Newton, T. (2001) *Improving Behaviour and Raising Self Esteem in the Classroom: A Practical Guide to Using Transactional Analysis*, David Fulton

Bradshaw, S. (2004) 'A curious condition', *Special*, Autumn

Campbell, D. (2002) *The Mozart Effect for Children*, Cygnus

Campbell. D. (2001) *Strengthen the Mind: Music for Intelligence and Learning* (Audio CD), Spring Hill Music

Canter, L. and M. (1976) *Assertive Discipline: Positive Behaviour Management for Today's Classroom*, Canter Associates

Collishaw, Stephan, *et al.* (2004), 'Time Trends in Adolescent Mental Health', *Journal of Child Psychology and Psychiatry*, 45 (8)

Cooper, C. (2002) *Understanding School Exclusion*, Education Now in association with Hull University

Devlin, A. (1997) *Criminal Classes*, Waterside

DfEE (1994) *The Education of Children with Emotional and Behavioural Problems*, circular 9/94

DfES (1989) *Discipline in Schools. Report of the Committee of Enquiry chaired by Lord Elton* (The Elton Report), HMSO

Ofsted (2005) *Managing Challenging Behaviour*, HMI report no. 2363

Ruiz, D.M. (1997) *The Four Agreements*, Amber Allen

Smith, Alistair (1996) *Accelerated Learning in the Classroom*, Network Educational Press

University of Birmingham (2005) *A Study of Young People Who Present Challenging Behaviour*, Ofsted. Available on the Ofsted website: www.ofsted.gov.uk

Wainwright, Gordon (2003) *Teach Yourself Body Language*, McGraw Hill